1

SCHOLASTIC

Reading & Math

This book belongs to

_____

Cover design by Sequel Creative
Cover art by Patrick Girouard
Interior illustrations by Abby Carter, Maxie Chambliss, Rusty Fletcher, James Graham Hale, Nicholas B. Lamia, Cindi, Ben, and Jim Mitchell, Sherry Neidigh, Peter Samek, Karen Sevaly, Carol Tiernon, and Patricia J. Wynne

ISBN 0-439-78600-2

1 2 3 4 5 6 7 8 9 10   56   25 24 23 22 21 20 19

Dear Parents,

The power to succeed is in every child! The question is: How can you help your child achieve this success and become an independent, lifelong learner?

You have already taken the first step! *Reading & Math* is the perfect way to support the learning your child needs to be successful in school.

Research shows that independent practice helps children gain mastery of essential skills. This book includes carefully selected, teacher-tested activities that give children in grade 1 exactly the practice they need. Topics covered include:

- Phonics
- Sight Words
- Handwriting
- Vocabulary
- Addition and Subtraction
- Time and Money

You'll also find assessments to help you keep track of your child's progress—and provide important practice with standardized test formats.

Let's get started! Your involvement will make this a valuable educational experience and will support and enhance your child's learning.

Enjoy!

Hindie

Hindie Weissman
Educational Consultant,
27+ years teaching experience

Welcome to *Reading & Math!*

Grade 1 is a critical stepping stone on the road to learning success! This workbook has been carefully designed to help ensure your child has the tools he or she needs to soar in school. On the 300-plus pages that follow, you'll find plenty of practice in each of these must-know curriculum areas:

ALPHABET	PHONICS/SPELLING	READING SKILLS	VOCABULARY
• Identifying Letters • Sequencing Letters • Writing Letters	• Identifying Consonants • Identifying Short & Long Vowel Spellings • Understanding Consonant Blends & Digraphs	• Recognizing Main Idea/Details • Recognizing Cause/Effect • Drawing Conclusions • Making Predictions	• Understanding Synonyms, Antonyms & Homophones • Using Content Area Words
GRAMMAR	**WRITING**	**NUMBERS**	**MATH CONCEPTS**
• Recognizing Types of Sentences • Understanding Parts of Speech	• Using Punctuation • Writing 3-Part Sentences • Writing Sequenced Directions • Naming a Story	• Understanding Addition • Understanding Subtraction	• Understanding Time • Understanding Money • Understanding Word Problems

Helping your child build essential skills is easy!

These teacher-approved activities have been specially developed to make learning both accessible and enjoyable. On each page, you'll find:

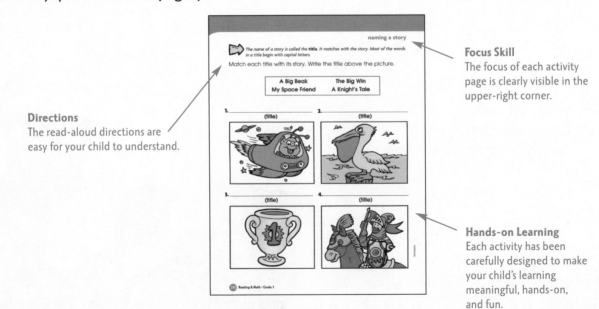

Directions
The read-aloud directions are easy for your child to understand.

Focus Skill
The focus of each activity page is clearly visible in the upper-right corner.

Hands-on Learning
Each activity has been carefully designed to make your child's learning meaningful, hands-on, and fun.

Scholastic

with Reading & Math!

These great extras are guaranteed to make learning extra engaging!

Reading & Math is loaded with lots of motivating, special components including:

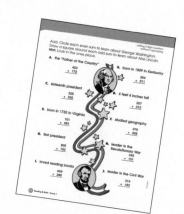

SPECIAL ACTIVITIES TO GET READY FOR SECOND GRADE

Give your child a head start in second grade with this BONUS assortment of get-ready activities.

CONNECTION TO ONLINE LEARNING

Boost computer literacy with this special link to a treasury of skill-building online activities at www.scholastic.com/success.

MOTIVATING STICKERS

Mark the milestones of your child's learning path with these bright, kid-pleasing stickers.

INSTANT FLASH CARDS

Promote reading fluency with these fun flash cards.

REWARD CERTIFICATE

Celebrate your child's leap in learning with this colorful, pull-out completion certificate.

LIST OF THE BEST BOOKS FOR YOUNG LEARNERS

Reinforce key concepts and build a love of reading with this great list of learning-rich books selected by top educators. See page 12.

QUICK ASSESSMENT TESTS

Make sure your child *really* masters each must-know skill with the instant assessment tests that conclude each section.

Table of Contents

Scholastic

MATHEMATICS

Scholastic

Scholastic

Tips for Success

Here are some tips to help your child get the most out of this workbook:

- Provide a quiet, comfortable place for your child to work.

- Make sure your child understands the directions.

- Encourage your child to use colorful pencils and markers to make learning fun.

- Check completed work as soon as possible and review corrected work with your child.

- Pay attention to areas where your child is having difficulty. Spend extra time to help him or her master those skills.

- Provide a special area at home where your child's work can be displayed.

- Be positive and encouraging. Praise your child for his or her efforts and good work.

Scholastic

Read with Your Child

Reading to your child and having him or her read to you is an extremely effective way of supporting your child's learning. When you read with him or her, make sure your child is actively participating. Here are five ways to support your child's reading:

1. Let your child choose the book.

2. Look at the cover of the book and ask your child what he or she thinks the story will be about.

3. As you read the book, locate a good stopping point and ask your child to predict what will happen next. Then read to confirm the prediction or correct it.

4. Discuss the characters in the story: Are they kind? good? bad? clever? Are they like characters in another book?

5. When you finish the story, have your child retell it.

Scholastic

Read with Your Child

Looking for a great book to read to your child? Here are some top teacher picks:

- *Alexander and the Wind-Up Mouse* by Leo Lionni (Knopf, 1969).

- *Click, Clack, Moo Cows That Type* by Doreen Cronin (Simon & Schuster, 2000).

- *David Goes to School* by David Shannon (Blue Sky Press, 2002).

- *Each Peach Pear Plum* by Janet and Allan Ahlberg (Viking Books, 1999).

- *Frog and Toad Together* by Arnold Lobel (HarperCollins, 1972).

- *Gregory, the Terrible Eater* by Mitchell Sharmat (Simon & Schuster, 1984).

- *The Mitten* by Jan Brett (Putnam, 1989).

- *Rosie's Walk* by Pat Hutchins (Simon & Schuster, 1968).

- *The Snowy Day* by Ezra Jack Keats (Viking Books, 1962).

- *Wemberly Worried* by Kevin Henkes (Greenwillow, 2000).

Scholastic

The Alphabet/Manuscript Handwriting

"Look, I'm writing words!" Once your child begins to put letters together to form words the magic of making words, and then sentences, begins.

In this section, your child will use upper- and lowercase letters of the alphabet to write sentences. Your child will also learn frequently used words, including the days of the week, the months of the year, and animal names.

What to Do

Encourage your child to trace and then write the letters and sentences on each page. Review his or her work. Compliment your child on carefully formed letters.

Keep On Going!

Have your child practice writing by having him or her write notes to family and friends. The notes might tell about a favorite movie or exciting plans coming up, such as a visit to the zoo.

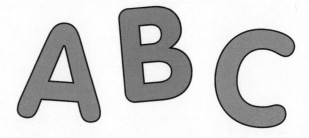

A a

Trace and write.

A   A   A

a   a   a

A a

Adam Ape is active.

Annie asked Alice.

B b

Trace and write.

B B B

b b b b

Bb Bb Bb

Betsy bee buzzes.

Betsy bee buzzes.

Bobby buys balloons.

Bobby buys balloons.

C c

Trace and write.

C C C C

c c c c

Cc

Cows crave color.

Callie carries cats.

D d

Trace and write.

D D D D D

d d d d

D d

Dandy Duck dances.

Dragons draw dogs.

Ee

Trace and write.

E E E E

e e e e

Ee

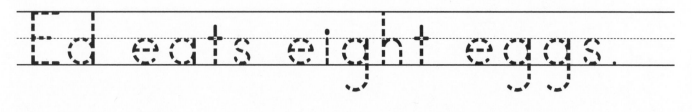

Ellie Emu is elegant.

Ed eats eight eggs.

F f

Trace and write.

F F F F

f f f f

F f

Fran Fish is funny.

Footballs fly fast.

G g

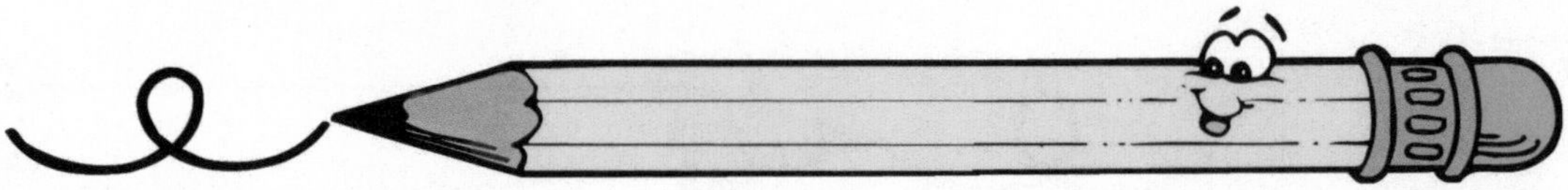

Trace and write.

G G G G

g g g g

Gg

Gus Goose giggles.

Greta grows greens.

Hee
Hee
Hee

Hh

Trace and write.

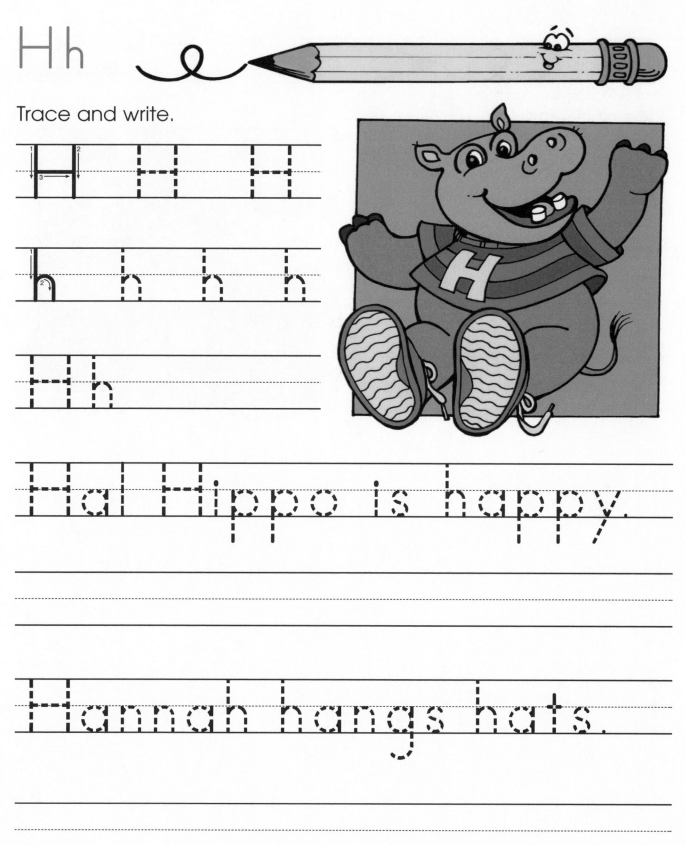

H H H H

h h h h

Hh

Hal Hippo is happy.

Hannah hangs hats.

I i

Trace and write.

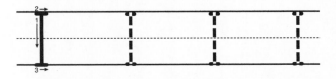

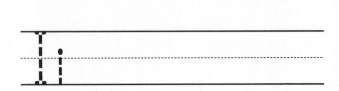

Irina Iguana is itchy.

Invite Irving inside.

Scholastic

Jj

Trace and write.

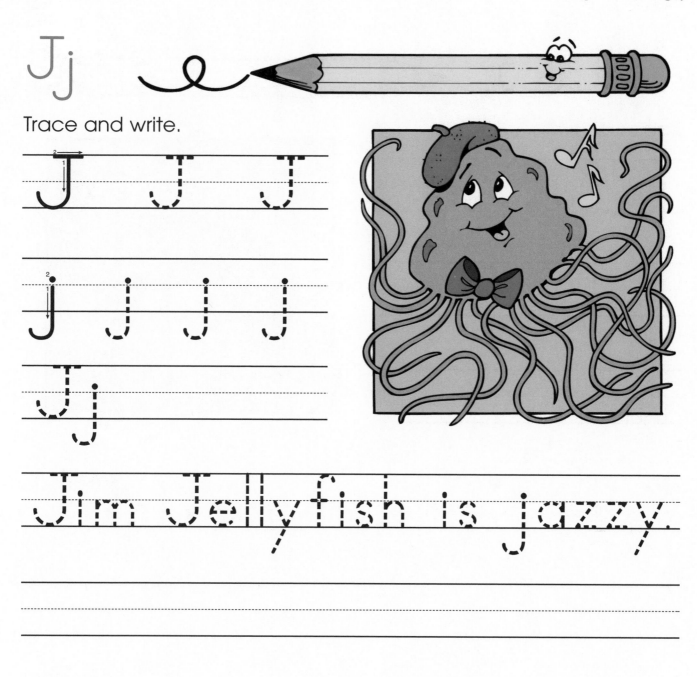

J J J J

j j j j

Jj

Jim Jellyfish is jazzy.

Jill juggles jelly jars.

K k

Trace and write.

K K K K

k k k k

K k

Kyle Kangaroo kicks.

Katie keeps kittens.

Scholastic

Ll

Trace and write.

L L L L L

I I I I I

L

Lyle Lion looks lost.

Lindy loves lollipops.

M m

Trace and write.

M M M

m m m

Mm

Mike Mouse is messy.

Mom met Madeline.

Scholastic

N n

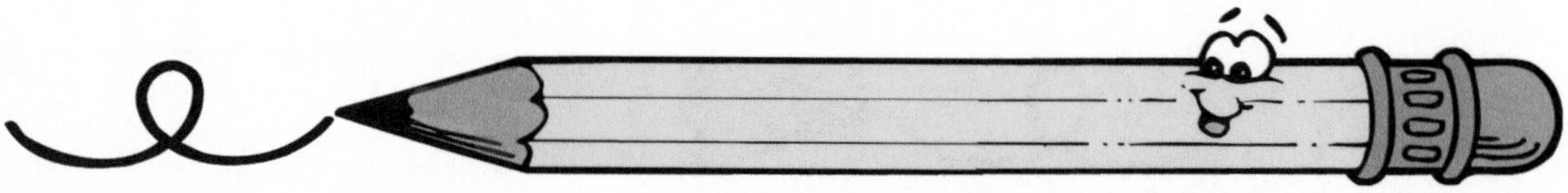

Trace and write.

N   N   N   N

n   n   n   n

Nn

Nikki Newt needs naps.

Nurse Ned nibbles.

O o

Trace and write.

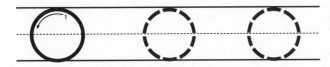

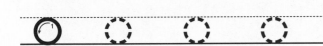

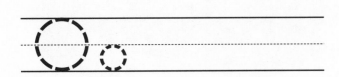

Opal Owl sings opera.

Otis orders oranges.

Scholastic

P p

Trace and write.

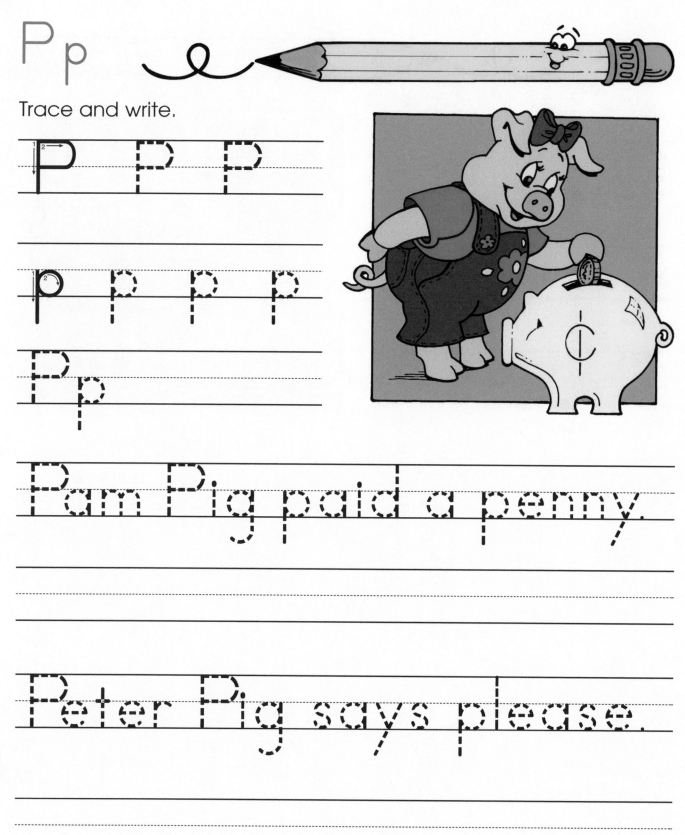

P P P P

p p p p

Pp

Pam Pig paid a penny.

Peter Pig says please.

Q q

Trace and write.

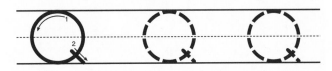

Qq

Quinn Quail is quiet.

Quebec is quite nice.

Scholastic

Rr

Trace and write.

R R R R

r r r r

Rr

Randy Rabbit races.

Robin reads rapidly.

S s

Trace and write.

S S S S S

s s s s s

Ss

Susanna Seal stars.

Sam sees sailboats.

Tt

Trace and write.

T T T T T

t t t t

T t

Tristan Toad is toothy.

Tigers taste terrible.

U u

Trace and write.

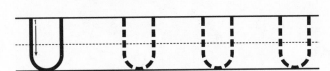

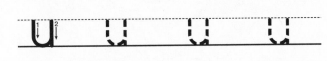

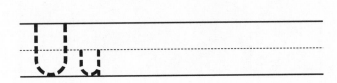

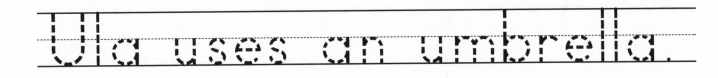

Ula uses an umbrella.

Uncle Uno umpires.

V v

Trace and write.

V V V V

v v v v

V v

Vic Vulture is vain.

Vegetables vary.

W w

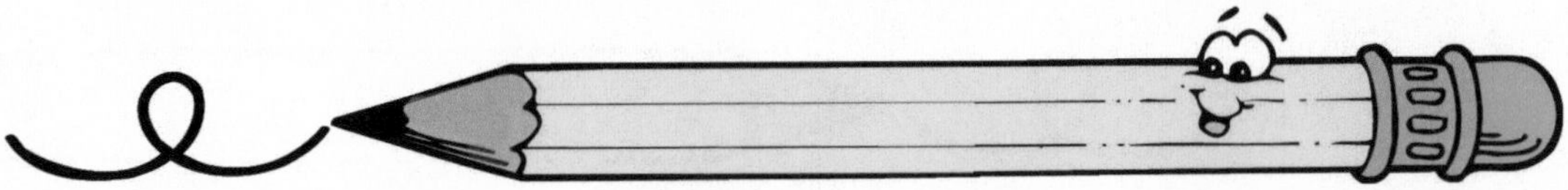

Trace and write.

W   W   W   W

w   w   w   w

Ww

Will Worm is wealthy.

Wilma wipes windows.

X x

Trace and write.

X X X X

X x x x x

X x

Xavier Fox is excited.

Xenia Ox exits.

Scholastic

Yy

Trace and write.

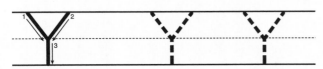

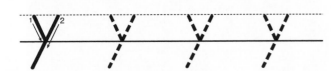

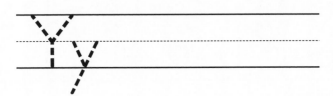

Yvonne Yak yawns.

Young yaks yodel.

Scholastic

Z z

Trace and write.

Z Z Z Z Z

z z z z z

Zz

Zoe Zebra is zany.

Zed zooms at the zoo.

Days of the Week

Trace and write.

Sunday

Monday

Tuesday

Wednesday

Thursday

Friday

Saturday

Scholastic

Months of the Year

Jan. Feb. March April May June

Trace and write.

January

February

March

April

May

June

Months of the Year

July   Aug.   Sept.   Oct.   Nov.   Dec.

Trace and write.

July

August

September

October

November

December

Scholastic

Animal Names

Write the animal names on the lines below.

alligator
bear

cougar
duck

frog
giraffe

Scholastic

Animal Names

Write the animal names on the lines below.

iguana   leopard

jaguar   moose

kangaroo   ostrich

_____

- - - - - - - - - - - - - - - - - - -

_____

- - - - - - - - - - - - - - - - - - -

_____

_____

- - - - - - - - - - - - - - - - - - -

_____

_____

- - - - - - - - - - - - - - - - - - -

_____

_____

- - - - - - - - - - - - - - - - - - -

_____

_____

- - - - - - - - - - - - - - - - - - -

_____

Animal Names

Write the animal names on the lines below.

parrot

quail

raccoon

squirrel

tiger

urchin

_____
- -
_____

_____
- -
_____

_____
- -
_____

_____
- -
_____

_____
- -
_____

Animal Names

Write the animal names on the lines below.

shark
vulture
whale

X-ray fish
yak
zebra

_____

- -

_____

- -

_____

- -

_____

- -

_____

- -

_____

- -

_____

Alphabet Practice Test

Fill in the bubble next to the correct answer.

Example

Say the word. Which letter is the first letter of the word?

○ d

○ c

● a

○ f

1. Say the word. Which letter is the first letter of the word?

○ t

○ e

○ r

○ d

2. Say the word. Which letter is the last letter of the word?

○ e

○ p

○ n

○ t

Alphabet Practice Test

Choose a sticker to place here.

Fill in the bubble next to the correct answer.

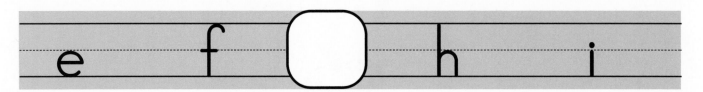

3. What letter is missing?

○ d

○ g

○ j

○ m

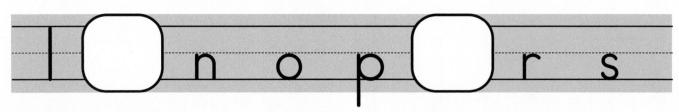

4. What two letters are missing?

○ m and q

○ t and g

○ m and t

○ q and u

Scholastic

Phonics/Spelling

Understanding the relationship between letters and the sounds they make, or phonics, is a giant step in learning to read. And a good grasp of phonics will help your child become a better speller.

What to Do

The activity pages in this section will give your child practice in identifying and spelling long- and short-vowel sounds, consonant blends, consonant digraphs, and rhyming words.

Have your child complete the activities on each page. Review the work together. Praise your child for a job well done!

Keep On Going!

Play a phonics/spelling game with your child. Set up word clues and ask your child to say and spell the word. For example:

> I start with the *bl* sound.
> I have a short-*o* vowel.
> I end with the *k* sound
> I rhyme with stock.
> What word am I? (block)

Have your child give you clues so you can guess the word.

There are 26 letters in the alphabet. Five of the letters are **vowels**;
A E I O U. All the rest are **consonants**.

Say each picture name and listen to the beginning sound. Find the
picture at the bottom of the page that has the same beginning
sound. Write the letter of the matching picture in the heart.

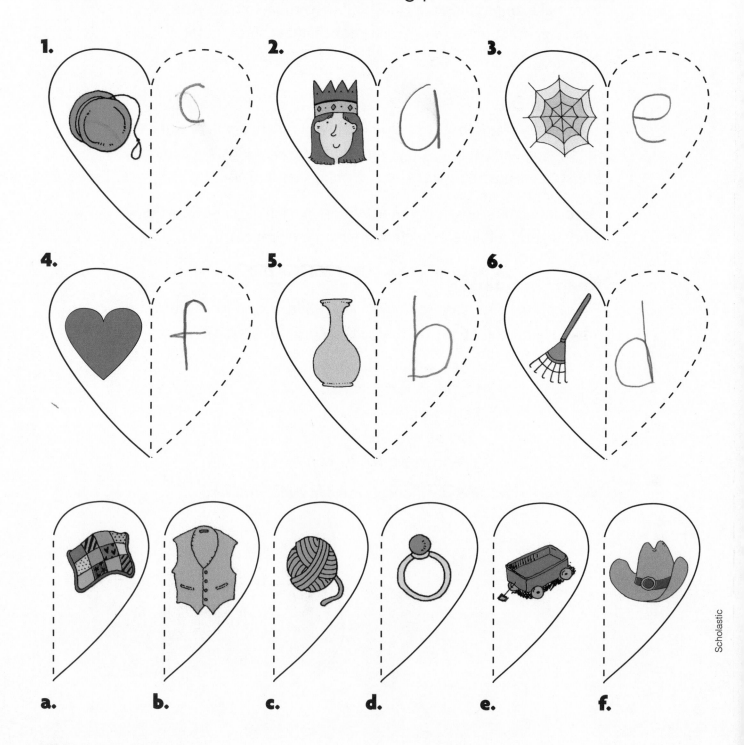

1. c

2. a

3. e

4. f

5. b

6. d

a.

b.

c.

d.

e.

f.

Scholastic

Say each animal name. Listen to the beginning sound. Find the animal at the bottom of the page that has the same beginning sound. Write the correct letter in each box.

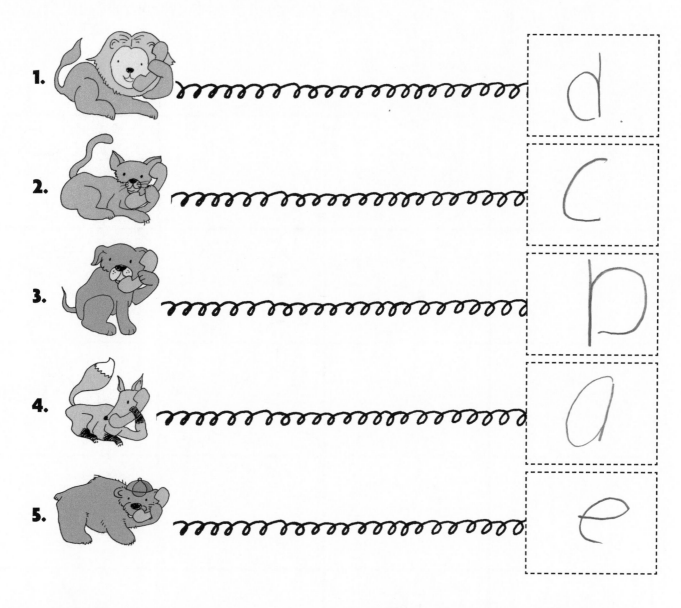

1.

2.

3.

4.

5.

a.   b.   c.   d.   e.

H *makes the sound you hear at the beginning of the words* **happy** *and* **hippo**.

Help Happy the hippo find the **h** words.
Say the picture in each box. Color
only the pictures that begin with **h**.

 This game begins with *h*. One child counts to ten and then tries to find the other children. Do you know what it is?

Scholastic

V *makes the sound you hear at the beginning of the words* **Vicki** *and* **vacation**.

Vicki is going on a vacation. Help Vicki load her van with things that start with **v**. Draw a line from the **v** words to the van.

K *makes the sound you hear at the beginning of the words* **Katie** *and* **kangaroo**.

Find and circle the pictures that begin with **k**.

Draw a line to the puzzle part that matches each clue.

1. It ends like

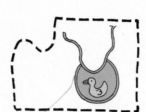

2. It ends like

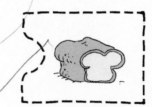

3. It ends like

4. It ends like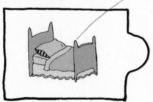

5. It ends like

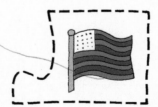

Scholastic

Match the pictures at the bottom of the page to each clue.
Write the words in the boxes.

1. It begins like  and ends like 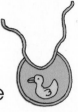 . **Cub**

2. It begins like and ends like . **Wig**

3. It begins like and ends like . **Pan**

4. It begins like and ends like . **Fox**

5. It begins like and ends like  . **leg**

Scholastic

Match each word at the bottom of the page to the word that has the same letters. Write the word in the box. Then write the letters that stand for the beginning and ending sound of each word. The first one has been done for you.

	Beginning Sound	Ending Sound
1. bus	b	s
sub		
	s	b
2. tip	t	p
pit	p	t
	t	n
3. ten	n	t
net	p	l
	l	p
4. pal	p	t
lap		
5. pot	p	p
top	t	s
	g	
6. gas	s	g
sag		

top   net   sag   pit   lap   sub

Scholastic

X *makes the sound of* ks. *(Hint: Say the word* kiss *very fast!) Most of the time, an* **x** *is in the middle or at the end of a word.*

Help Superhero X put the missing **x** in each word. Then draw a line to the matching picture.

fo___

mi___er

ta___i

e___it

a___

si___

o___

bo___

e___ercise

tu___edo

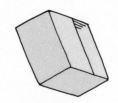

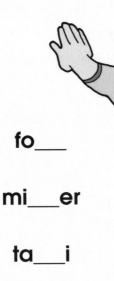

Scholastic

Sometimes a consonant may make no sound at all. For example, when k and n come together, the k is silent. When w and r come together, the w is silent. When r and h come together, the h is silent.

Look at the words and pictures. Make a sleepy eye, like this: above the consonant that is silent. Do not color it. Then color the other letters in the word.

knife

knot

knock

knit

wreck

write

wreath

wrist

rhinoceros

Scholastic

Read to find out why these children got in trouble. Circle all the double consonants in each sentence. Then find the picture that goes with the sentence. Write the number of the sentence in the correct box.

1. William and Jesse giggled in class.

2. Emma and Jenna scribbled on the wall.

3. Hannah and Kelly tattled to Mommy.

4. Connor and Kenny held a muddy puppy.

Scholastic

Rhyming words *sound alike. They are made by changing only the beginning sound of a word. The rest of the word stays the same.*

Each word puzzle below shows how to make a rhyming word. The first one has been done for you.

1.  ~~m~~an – m + f = <u>fan</u>

2. hook – h + b = _____

3.  cake – c + r = _____

4.  dog – d + l = _____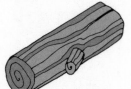

5.  tire – t + f = _____

6. well – w + b = _____

7.  king – k + r = _____

Make your own rhyming words. Look at the picture and say the word. Copy the word. Then change the first letter using each of the letters on the hammer to make new words.

h c m t w f

p s r m f h b

s l b

f j l h

ball

cat

hand

dog

Scholastic

Poems are made with rhyming words. Read the Mother Goose rhymes. Find a word from the Word Box below to rhyme with each underlined word. Copy the word on the line.

1. Jack and <u>Jill</u>

Went up the _____

To fetch a pail of water.

Jack fell <u>down</u>

And broke his _____,

And Jill came tumbling after.

3. Hickory dickory <u>dock</u>

The mouse ran up the

_____.

The clock struck one,

The mouse ran down

Hickory dickory dock.

2. Hey diddle <u>diddle</u>

The cat and the _____,

The cow jumped

over the <u>moon</u>.

The little dog laughed

to see such sport,

And the dish ran

away with the _____.

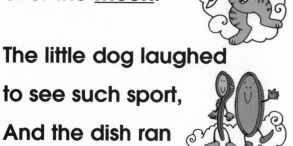

4. Mary had a little lamb,

Its fleece was white

as _____.

Everywhere that Mary went,

The lamb was sure to <u>go</u>.

Word Box

| fiddle | snow | crown | clock | hill | spoon |

A. Use a list word to complete each sentence.

List Words: | at | had | an | can | as | and |

1. We went to _____ apple farm.

2. We picked green _____ red apples.

3. One apple was as big _____ a ball.

4. We _____ lots of fun!

5. We went home _____ dinnertime.

6. Now Mom _____ make apple pie.

B. Each list word is hidden two times. Circle the words.

hidanaastcan

kuhadtatiand

ashadinande

dahcaniatean

 C. Write the challenge word that matches each clue.

| lamp | fast |

I can be turned off and on. I am a _____.

I am not slow. I am _____.

The **short-***e* **sound** *is the beginning sound of the word* **elephant**.

A. Read each list word. Circle the letter that makes the short-*e* sound.

 Read.   **Copy.**   **Organize.**

list words with *en*

Read	Copy	
1. end	**1.** _____	
2. get	**2.** _____	_____
3. let	**3.** _____	_____
4. red	**4.** _____	list words with *et*
5. ten	**5.** _____	_____
6. yes	**6.** _____	_____

 Challenge Words

other list words

7. nest	**7.** _____	_____
8. went	**8.** _____	_____

B. Write the list word that begins with the same sound as each picture.

 **1.**  _____   **2.**  _____   **3.**  _____

4. _____   **5.** _____   **6.** 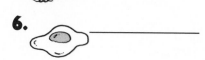 _____

The **short-**i **sound** *is the beginning sound for the word* **inchworm**.

A. Read each list word. Circle the letter that makes the short-*i* sound.

Read.

1. if

2. is

3. big

4. him

5. his

6. sit

Challenge Words

7. will

8. flip

Copy.

1. _____

2. _____

3. _____

4. _____

5. _____

6. _____

7. _____

8. _____

Organize.

list words that begin with *i*

_____

_____

list words that begin with *h*

_____

_____

other list words

_____

_____

B. Write the list word that ends with the same sound as each picture.

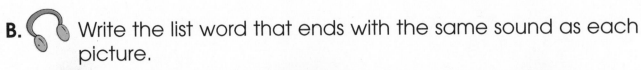

1.  _____

2.  _____

3.  _____

4. _____

5. 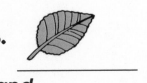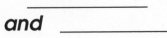 _____ *and* _____

The **short-o sound** *is the beginning sound of the word* **octopus.**

A. Read each list word. Circle the letter that makes the short-*o* sound.

 Read.   **Copy.**   **Organize.**

Read.	Copy.	Organize.
1. on	**1.** _____	list words with *op*
2. got	**2.** _____	_____
3. hop	**3.** _____	_____
4. fox	**4.** _____	list words with *ot*
5. top	**5.** _____	_____
6. not	**6.** _____	_____

 Challenge Words

other list words

7. rock	**7.** _____	_____
8. stop	**8.** _____	

B. Write the list word that matches each picture.

1.  _____   **2.**  _____

3. _____   **4.**  _____

The **short-u sound** *is the beginning sound of the word* **umbrella**.

A. Read each list word. Circle the letter that makes the short-*u* sound.

Read.

1. up
2. but
3. run
4. bug
5. mud
6. jump

🏆 **Challenge Words**

7. funny
8. puppy

✏️ **Copy.**

1. _____
2. _____
3. _____
4. _____
5. _____
6. _____

7. _____
8. _____

🔤 **Organize.**

two-letter list word

_____

three-letter list words

_____

_____

_____

_____

_____

four-letter list word

_____

B.  Write the list word that rhymes with each word.

1. bud _____   2. lump _____   3. hut _____

4. sun _____   5. tug _____   6. cup _____

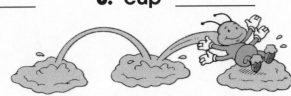

Scholastic

The **long**-a **sound** can be spelled with the letters *ay* like in the word **may** and the letters *ai* like in the word **mail**.

A. Read each list word. Circle the letters that make the long-*a* sound.

 Read.

1. day
2. rain
3. tail
4. play
5. wait
6. stay

 Challenge Words

7. away
8. chain

Copy.

1. _____
2. _____
3. _____
4. _____
5. _____
6. _____

7. _____
8. _____

 Organize.

list words with long-*a* sound spelled *ay*

_____
_____
_____

list words with long-*a* sound spelled *ai*

_____
_____
_____

B. Write the list word that begins with the same sound as the picture.

1. _____
2. _____
3. _____

4. _____
5. _____
6.  _____

The **long**-e **sound** *can also be spelled with the letter* e *like in the word* **he** *and the letters* ee *like in the word* **need**.

A. Read each list word. Circle the letters that make the long-*e* sound.

Read.

1. me
2. tree
3. we
4. need
5. see
6. feet

 **Challenge Words**

7. sleep
8. sheep

Copy.

1. _____
2. _____
3. _____
4. _____
5. _____
6. _____

7. _____
8. _____

Organize.

list words with long-*e* sound spelled *ee*

_____
_____
_____
_____

list words with long-*e* sound spelled *e*

_____
_____

B.  Write the list word that begins with the same sound as each picture.

1. _____   2.  _____   3.  _____

4.  _____   5. _____   6.  _____

Scholastic

The **long-**i **sound** is can be spelled with the letters i_e like in the word **ice** and the letter y like in the word **try**.

A. Read each list word. Circle the letter that makes the long-*i* sound.

 Read.

1. by
2. like
3. I
4. my
5. kite
6. fly

 Copy.

1. _____
2. _____
3. _____
4. _____
5. _____
6. _____

 Organize.

list words with *i_e*

_____

_____

_____

list words with *y*

_____

_____

_____

the shortest list word

_____

 Challenge Words

7. time
8. hi

7. _____
8. _____

B. Write the list word that rhymes with each picture.

1.  _____   2. _____

C. Write four list words that rhyme with each other.

_____   _____   _____   _____

*The **long-**o **sound** is sometimes spelled with the letter* o *like in the word **no** and the letters* o_e *like in the word **cone**.*

A. Read each list word. Circle the letters that make the long-*o* sound.

 Read.

 Copy.

 Organize.

1. so

2. home

3. go

4. bone

5. note

6. rope

1. _____

2. _____

3. _____

4. _____

5. _____

6. _____

list words with long-*o* sound spelled *o_e*

_____

_____

_____

_____

 Challenge Words

7. vote

8. stone

7. _____

8. _____

list words with long-*o* sound spelled *o*

_____

_____

B.  Write the list word with the same ending sound as each picture.

1.  _____

2.  _____

3.  _____

4. _____

5. _____   *and* _____

The **consonant-vowel-consonant-silent e rule:** *When a word ends in a silent* e, *the vowel that comes before the* e *will be long and will say its name.*

Mr. Mule has all the answers! He wants you to choose one of his words to complete each sentence. Write the word on the blank.

chute huge rude
dune flute June
cute

1. It is _____ to talk back to your mother.

2. She plays the _____ in the band.

3. Throw your dirty socks down the clothes _____.

4. It is fun to roll down a big sand _____.

5. The giant had _____ feet!

6. My birthday is in _____.

7. This baby is so _____!

Scholastic

A **consonant blend** *is when two consonants are side by side in a word and you hear both sounds blended together.* **Fl** *makes the sound you hear at the beginning of the words* **Flora** *and* **flower**.

Flora loves to plant flowers. Her favorite ones are yellow flowers. Color the pictures that begin with *fl* yellow. Color all the other pictures orange.

Fr *makes the sound you hear at the beginning of* **Freddy** *and* **friend**.

This is a picture of Freddy's friend. Her name is Fran. There are nine things in this picture that begin with **fr**. Draw a red circle around each one.

fruit	frame	French fries	fringe

frog	frown	freezer	freckles	frosting

Gl *makes the sound you hear at the beginning of the words* **Glen** *and* **Gloria**.

Glen and Gloria want to ask you some questions. Read each question below. Then find the answer in the Word Box and write it on the blank.

1. What is another word for happy?

_____

2. What kind of airplane is this?

_____

3. What should I add to make my picture sparkle?

_____

4. I cannot see the board. What do I need?

_____

5. How can I find out where Africa is?

_____

6. How will I keep my hands warm?

_____

7. What will make my lips shine?

_____

8. How can I fix this?

_____

Word Box

 glasses glider  glue globe

lip gloss glad gloves glitter

Scholastic

Sn *makes the sound you hear at the beginning of the words* **Sniffles** *and* **snake**.

Why is Sniffles the snake crying? He is lost! Help him find his way back to his mother. First, color only the pictures that begin with **sn**. Then use those clues to draw the path to Sniffles' mother.

Scholastic

Sm *makes the sound you hear at the beginning of the words* **Smiley** *and* **Smith**.

Help Smiley Smith find the correct answers. He is looking for one picture in each row that begins with **sm**. Draw a smiley face in each box whose picture begins with **sm**.

1.

2.

3.

Scholastic

St *makes the sound you hear at the beginning of the words* **Stella** *and* **stars**.

Stella has made up a game for you! Use the star code to make words that begin with **st**. Write the correct letter above each star. Then draw a line to match each word you made to the correct picture.

A	C	E	F	H	I	K	L	M	O	P	R	S	T	V

1. _ _ _ _ _

2. _ _ _ _ _

3. _ _ _ _ _ _ _

4. _ _ _ _ _

5. _ _ _ _ _ _ _ _

6. _ _ _ _ _ _ _

7. _ _ _ _ _

8. _ _ _ _ _ _

Scholastic

Tw *makes the sound you hear at the beginning of the words* **Twila** *and* **twins**.

Twila's twins love to ask questions. Read each question below. Find a word that answers the question and write it in the correct bubble.

Tweezers	Tweet! Tweet!	Twelve	Twirl!	Twister	Twenty

Scholastic

Str *makes the sound you hear at the beginning of the word* **strike**.

Look at the pictures on the baseball caps below. If the picture begins with **str**, make red stripes on the cap. If the picture does not begin with **str**, color the whole cap yellow.

Scholastic

When two consonants come together and make one new sound, these consonant letters are called **digraphs**.

Look at the man making new sounds in the digraph machine. He puts in two letters, but only one sound comes out!

Sh!

Now you try it! Look at the two letters. When the word comes out at the end, draw a green circle around the two letters that make the new sound. That is the digraph!

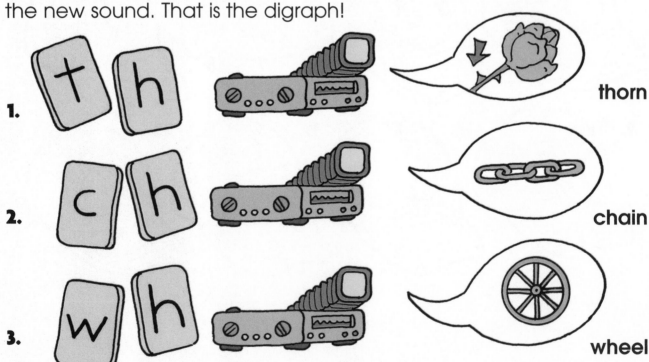

1. t h — thorn

2. c h — chain

3. w h — wheel

Scholastic

The letters **th** *make the sound at the beginning of the word* **thorn**.

A. Read each list word. Circle the letters *th* in each word.

 Read.

1. the

2. this

3. with

4. then

5. bath

6. that

Copy.

1. _____

2. _____

3. _____

4. _____

5. _____

6. _____

Organize.

list words that begin with *th*

_____

_____

_____

_____

list words that end with *th*

_____

_____

🏆 **Challenge Words**

7. them

8. they

7. _____

8. _____

B. Write the list word that rhymes with each word.

1. math _____   2. den _____   3. rat _____

👀 Unscramble each list word.

4. het _____   5. hiwt _____   6. tsih _____

*The letters **sh** make the sound at the beginning of the word **shell**.*

A. Read each list word. Circle the letters *sh* in each word.

 Read.   **Copy.**   **Organize.**

list words that begin with *sh*

	Read.		Copy.
1.	ship	**1.**	_____
2.	she	**2.**	_____
3.	fish	**3.**	_____
4.	shape	**4.**	_____
5.	wish	**5.**	_____
6.	brush	**6.**	_____

_____

_____

_____

list words that end with *sh*

 Challenge Words

_____

7.	shine	**7.**	_____
8.	shoe	**8.**	_____

_____

_____

B. Draw a (shell) around the list word that is spelled correctly.

1.	shipe	ship	**2.**	shape	shap	**3.**	she	shee
4.	fish	fich	**5.**	brosh	brush	**6.**	wich	wish

Scholastic

The letters **ch** *make the sound at the beginning of the word* **chain**. *The letters* **wh** *make the sound at the beginning of the word* **wheel**.

A. Read each list word. Circle the letters *ch* and *wh* in each word.

Read.

1. chin

2. chop

3. whale

4. when

5. inch

6. which

🏆 **Challenge Words**

7. why

8. what

Copy.

1. _____

2. _____

3. _____

4. _____

5. _____

6. _____

7. _____

8. _____

Organize.

list words that begin with *ch*

_____

_____

list words that begin with *wh*

_____

_____

_____

list words that end with *ch*

_____

_____

B. Write the list word that rhymes with each word.

1. tail _____

2. mop _____

3. pinch _____

4. pitch _____

5. pen _____

6. win _____

The letters **ck** *make the sound at the end of the word* **pick**.

A. Read each list word. Circle the letters *ck* in each word.

 Read.　　 **Copy.**　　 **Organize.**

list words with short-*a* sound

1. duck　　1. _____　　_____

2. pack　　2. _____　　_____

3. stick　　3. _____　　list word with short-*e* sound

4. back　　4. _____　　_____

5. neck　　5. _____　　list word with short-*i* sound

6. rock　　6. _____　　_____

 Challenge Words　　list word with short-*o* sound

_____

7. clock　　7. _____　　list word with short-*u* sound

8. quick　　8. _____　　_____

B.  Write the list word that matches each picture.

1.  _____　　2.  _____　　3. _____

4. _____　　5.  _____　　6. 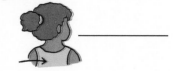 _____

Scholastic

The letters **ar** *make the sound at the beginning of the word* **arch**.

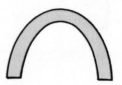

A. Read each list word. Circle the letters *ar* in each word.

Read.

1. are

2. hard

3. star

4. jar

5. part

6. farm

🏆 **Challenge Words**

7. start

8. shark

✏️ **Copy.**

1. _____

2. _____

3. _____

4. _____

5. _____

6. _____

7. _____

8. _____

🧱 **Organize.**

list words with *ar* in the middle

_____

_____

_____

other list words

_____

_____

_____

B. 🎧 Write the list word that rhymes with each word.

1. card _____

2. art _____

3. harm _____

4. car _____ *and* _____ *and* _____

The letters **or** *make the sound at the beginning of the word* **ornament.**

A. Read each list word. Circle the letters *or* in each word.

 Read.

1. or

2. corn

3. porch

4. horn

5. for

6. short

 Challenge Words

7. your

8. horse

 Copy.

1. _____

2. _____

3. _____

4. _____

5. _____

6. _____

7. _____

8. _____

 Organize.

two- or three-letter list words

_____

_____

four- or five-letter list words

_____

_____

_____

_____

_____

B.  Write the list word that begins with the same sound as each picture.

1. _____ **2.** _____ **3.** _____

4. _____ **5.** _____ **6.** _____

Scholastic

Throughout the year, see if you can learn all the words on this Grade 1 spelling list.

an	do	if	or	tape
and	dog	inch	pack	ten
are	duck	is	park	that
arm	end	jar	part	the
as	farm	jump	play	then
at	feet	kite	porch	this
ate	fish	let	rain	thorn
back	fly	like	red	to
bath	for	love	rock	top
big	fork	make	rope	tray
black	fox	math	run	tree
bone	from	me	see	up
brush	gave	men	seed	wait
bug	get	mud	shape	we
but	go	my	she	whale
by	got	nail	ship	when
cake	had	name	shop	which
came	hand	neck	short	white
can	hard	need	sit	wish
car	hat	nine	six	with
chin	him	north	so	yes
chip	his	nose	star	you
chop	home	not	stay	
corn	hop	note	stick	
day	horn	of	sun	
dish	I	on	tail	

Phonics/Spelling Practice Test

Fill in the bubble next to the correct answer.

1. Which word has the long-*a* sound?

    ○ **A**   dart

    ○ **B**   man

    ○ **C**   made

    ○ **D**   Mary

2. Which word has the short-*e* sound?

    ○ **F**   seed

    ○ **G**   men

    ○ **H**   teeth

    ○ **J**   eye

3. Which word does not have the long-*a* sound?

    ○ **A**   pail

    ○ **B**   boat

    ○ **C**   cake

    ○ **D**   play

Scholastic

Phonics/Spelling Practice Test

Fill in the bubble next to the correct answer.

4. Which word rhymes with love?

○ **A**   come

○ **B**   from

○ **C**   dove

○ **D**   some

5. Which word rhymes with high?

○ **F**   fright

○ **G**   sight

○ **H**   sigh

○ **J**   night

6. Which word answers the following riddle?

I shine in the sky. What am I?

○ **A**   Mars

○ **B**   star

○ **C**   Earth

○ **D**   Saturn

Phonics/Spelling Practice Test

Fill in the bubble next to the correct answer.

7. Which word does not have the long-*e* sound?

○ **A** monkey

○ **B** made

○ **C** feet

○ **D** baby

8. Which word rhymes with kind?

○ **F** mine

○ **G** find

○ **H** fine

○ **J** child

9. Which word has the short-*i* sound?

○ **A** line

○ **B** lit

○ **C** lime

○ **D** light

Scholastic

Phonics/Spelling Practice Test

Fill in the bubble next to the correct answer.

10. Which word does not have the long-*u* sound?

○ **A**   fur

○ **B**   cute

○ **C**   huge

○ **D**   June

11. Which word has a short-vowel sound?

○ **F**   ride

○ **G**   rot

○ **H**   right

○ **J**   read

12. Which word has a long-vowel sound?

○ **A**   flick

○ **B**   flip

○ **C**   fry

○ **D**   flap

Scholastic

Reading Skills &
Reading Comprehension

In this section, your child reviews previously learned reading skills and is introduced to new ones. These essential skills will help your child better comprehend what he or she is reading.

What to Do
Read each page with your child. Then have him or her complete the activities. Be sure to review your child's work.

Keep On Going!
Have your child choose a book he or she wants to read and read it together. Start by asking your child to look at the cover of the book. Have him or her predict what the story will be about based on the cover picture. Next, while reading, stop every few pages and ask questions such as: "Where did the story take place?" "Describe the main characters." "What do you think will happen next?" "What problem does the main character face?" "How is the problem solved?" "Retell the story in your own words." This process is called active reading. Good readers are active readers!

Tim is a good reader. He uses clues to help him read. First, he looks at the pictures. That helps him know what the story is about. Next, he reads the title of the story. Now he knows a little more. As he reads the story, the words make pictures in his mind.

Color in the book beside the correct answer.

1. Who is Tim?

 a good reader   a math whiz

2. What does Tim do first?

 reads the story   looks at the pictures

3. What else helps Tim know what the story will be about?

 the title   the page number

4. As he reads, what makes pictures in Tim's mind?

 the letters   the words

The **main idea** *tells what the whole story is about.*

Today I went to the circus. My favorite part of the circus was the clowns. Clowns can do funny tricks. A clown named Pinky turned flips on the back of a horse. Fancy Pants juggled balls while he was singing a funny song. Happy Hal made balloons into animal shapes. Then twelve clowns squeezed into a tiny car and rode away.

Color in the ball that tells the main idea.

Pinky rides a horse.

Balloons can be shaped like animals.

Clowns can do funny tricks.

Clowns drive tiny cars.

Fancy Pants sang a song.

Trucks do important work. Dump trucks carry away sand and rocks. Cement trucks have a barrel that turns round and round. They deliver cement to workers who are making sidewalks. Fire trucks carry water hoses and firefighters. Gasoline is delivered in large tank trucks. Flatbed trucks carry wood to the people who are building houses.

Find the sentence in the story that tells the main idea. Write it in the circle below. Then draw a line from the main idea to all the trucks that were described in the story.

When you were born, your parents thought of a name for you. You might be named after someone in the family. Maybe you were named after a movie star! Almost every name has a meaning. Pamela means "honey." Henry means "master of the house." Ellen means "bright." Sometimes books about baby names tell the meanings. Many of the meanings will surprise you!

A. Circle the name below that has the main idea of the story in it.

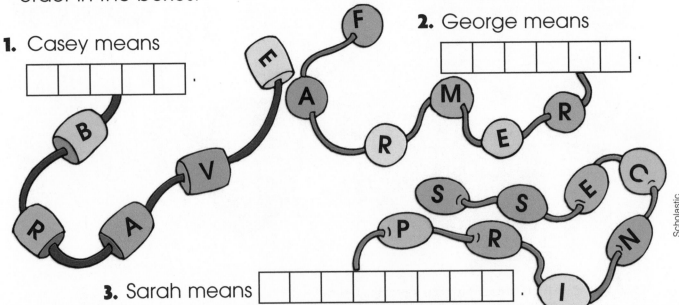

B. To find out the meanings of the names in the puzzle below, follow each string of beads. Copy the letters on each bead in order in the boxes.

1. Casey means

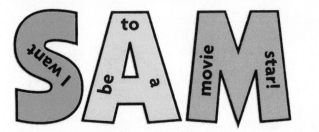

2. George means

3. Sarah means

Scholastic

Details *are parts of a story. Details help you understand what the story is about.*

Skunks are small animals that live in the woods. They have black fur with one or two white stripes down their backs. Bugs are their favorite food. They also eat mice. If a skunk raises its tail, run away! Skunks can spray a very smelly liquid at anyone who bothers them.

Write the answers in the crossword puzzle.

Across

2. What color are the stripes on a skunk's fur?

5. What is a skunk's favorite food?

Down

1. What is another thing that skunks like to eat?

2. Where do skunks live?

3. What does a skunk raise when it is getting ready to spray?

4. What should you do if a skunk raises its tail?

Use details to describe your favorite animal.

Ricky loved to go camping. One day during reading class, he began to daydream about camping in the mountains. He thought about going fishing and riding horses. It would be fun to gather logs to build a campfire and cook hot dogs. He and his dad could set up the tent near some big trees. He wished he were in his canoe right now. Just then, Ricky heard his teacher say, "Ricky, it is your turn to read." Oh no! He had lost the place!

Circle these things from the story hidden in the picture below: a fish, a fishing pole, a log for the campfire, a hot dog, a tree, and a canoe.

1. Where was Ricky during this story? _____

_____

2. Where would Ricky like to have been? _____

_____

Kelly is going to spend the night with her grandmother. She will need to take her pajamas, a shirt, and some shorts. Into the suitcase go her toothbrush, toothpaste, and hairbrush. Grammy told her to bring a swimsuit in case it was warm enough to swim. Mom said to pack her favorite pillow and storybooks. Dad said, "Don't forget to take Grammy's sunglasses that she left here last week." Now Kelly is ready to go!

1. Color the things that Kelly packed in her suitcase.

2. A compound word is a big word that is made up of two little words. For example, cow + boy = cowboy. Find 8 compound words in this story and circle them.

Scholastic

Sequencing *means putting the events in a story in the order they happened.*

Last summer I learned how to swim. First, the teacher told me to hold my breath. Then I learned to put my head under water. I practiced kicking my feet. While I held on to a float, I paddled around the pool. Next, I floated to my teacher with my arms straight out. Finally, I swam using both my arms and my legs. I did it! Swimming is fun! This summer, I want to learn to dive off the diving board.

Number the pictures in the order that they happened in the story.

Unscramble the letters to tell what the boy in the story wants to do next.

EALNR   **OT**   **IVDE**

___ ___ ___ ___ ___   ___ ___   ___ ___ ___ ___

1. Read the story.

My mother gave me some seeds. I dug some holes in the garden. I planted the seeds.

Each day I watered the seeds. I waited for a few weeks to go by. Soon some flowers began to grow.

2. Read the sentences below. Rewrite them in the correct order.

Some flowers began to grow.

I planted the seeds.

My mother gave me some seeds.

I watered the seeds.

1. _____

2. _____

3. _____

4. _____

Scholastic

1. Read the story.

Tomorrow I will go swimming. I will put on my swimsuit. I will jump in the water to get wet. Then I will dive off of the diving board. Grandma will fix lunch for me. Mom will swim with me after lunch.

2. Read the sentences below. Rewrite them in the correct order.

Mom will swim with me.

I will put on my swimsuit.

Grandma will fix lunch for me.

I will jump in the water.

1. _____

2. _____

3. _____

4. _____

Scholastic

1. Read the story.

Dad and I went fishing today. We woke up very early. We ate breakfast. We left the house after we ate. We went to the bait store. Dad bought some worms. We caught five fish. Mom was happy to cook them for us.

2. Read the sentences below. Rewrite them in the correct order.

We ate breakfast.

Dad bought some bait.

We woke up early.

Mom cooked our fish.

1. _____

_____

2. _____

_____

3. _____

_____

4. _____

Scholastic

Use story details to make a guess about what will happen next.

Mia and Rosa were playing hospital. Mia was the patient, and Rosa was the doctor. Rosa pretended to take Mia's temperature. "You have a fever," she said. "You will have to lie down." Mia climbed onto the top bunk bed. "You need to sleep," Dr. Rosa said. Mia rolled over too far and fell off the top bunk. "O-o-o-h, my arm!" yelled Mia. Her mother came to look. It was broken!

What do you think happened next? Write your answer here.

_____

To find out if your answer is correct, finish the sentence below by coloring only the spaces that have a dot in them.

Mia had to go to

Scholastic

One day, Sam was riding his bike to the baseball game. He had to be on time. He was the pitcher. Just ahead, Sam saw a little boy who had fallen off his bike. His knee was bleeding, and he was crying. Sam asked him if he was okay, but the boy was crying too much to speak. Sam knew the boy needed help getting home. If he stopped to help, he might be late for the game. Sam thought about it. He knew he had to do the right thing.

What do you think Sam did next? There are two paths through the maze. Draw a line down the path that shows what you think Sam did next.

What sentence from the story gives you a hint about what Sam decided to do? Write that sentence below.

_____

Picturing a story can help the reader understand it better.

An artist drew the pictures that are in this book. Now it is your turn to be the artist! Read each sentence very carefully. Draw exactly what you read about in the sentence.

1. The green and yellow striped snake wiggled past the ants.

2. Wildflowers grew along the banks of the winding river.

3. On her sixth birthday, Shannon had a pink birthday cake shaped like a butterfly.

Scholastic

Big, black clouds appeared in the sky. Lightning struck the tallest tree. The scared cow cried, "Moo!" It rained hard. Soon there was a mud puddle by the barn door. Hay blew out of the barn window.

Read the story above. Then go back and read each sentence again. Add to the picture everything that the sentences describe.

Scholastic

Grouping like things together makes it easier to remember what you read.

Mom says, "Let's go out for ice cream! Clean your room, and then we will go." Your room is a mess. You need to put the blocks in the basket. The crayons must go in their box. The books must go on the shelf, and the marbles go in the jar. You can do it. Just think about that hot fudge sundae!

Draw a line from each item on the floor to the place it belongs. Color red the things that you could use in school. Color the toys blue.

Circle the food that does not belong in an ice cream store.

Scholastic

Look for similarities when grouping items.

Read the words in the Word Box. Write each word in the place where you would find these things at the mall.

Word Box

tickets	sandals	high heels	beans	big screen
tulip bulbs	peppers	fertilizer	popcorn	gardening gloves
sneakers	burritos	boots	pots	candy	tacos

Sandie's Shoe Store

1.

Movie Town Cinema

2.

PEPE'S MEXICAN FOOD

3.

Gale's Gardening Goodies

4.

Eating good food helps you grow up to be strong and healthy. There are many kinds of foods. Ham, chicken, and beef are meats. Dairy foods include milk, cheese, and yogurt. What kinds of bread do you like? I like muffins, bagels, and biscuits. Fruits and vegetables, such as carrots, corn, and apples, are good for you. They are full of vitamins.

Look at the pictures of different foods below. Draw a line from each food to the category it belongs to.

Meats	Dairy	Breads

Fruits and Vegetables

Scholastic

Compare *means to look for things that are the same.*
Contrast *means to look for things that are different.*

To solve the riddles in each box, read the clues in the horse.
Then write the letters in the blanks with the matching numbers.

What kind of food does a racehorse like to eat?

___ ___ ___ ___   ___ ___ ___ ___
11   5   10   3   11   9   9   2

1. What letter is in LOG, but not in DOG?
2. What letter is in DIME, but not in TIME?
3. What letter is in BITE, but not in BIKE?
4. What letter is in WEST, but not in REST?
5. What letter is in FAN, but not in FUN?
6. What letter is in BOX, but not in FOX?
7. What letter is in CAR, but not in CAN?
8. What letter is in ME, but not in MY?
9. What letter is in SOCK, but not in SACK?
10. What letter is in SEE, but not in BEE?
11. What letter is in FULL, but not in PULL?

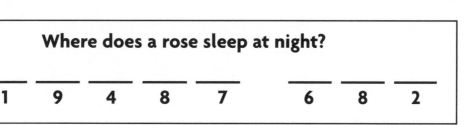

Where does a rose sleep at night?

___ ___ ___ ___ ___ ___   ___ ___ ___
11   1   9   4   8   7   6   8   2

Holly and Polly are twins. They are in the first grade. They look just alike, but they are very different. Holly likes to play softball and soccer. She likes to wear her hair braided when she goes out to play. She wears sporty clothes. Recess is her favorite part of school. Polly likes to read books and paint pictures. Every day she wears a ribbon in her hair to match her dress. Her favorite thing about school is going to the library. She wants to be a teacher some day.

Look at the pictures of Holly and Polly. Their faces look alike. Circle the things in both pictures that are different from each other.

Draw two lines under the words that tell what Holly and Polly do that is the same.

They play sports.   They love to paint.   They are in the first grade.

Scholastic

Juan's dad and Ann's dad are soldiers. Juan's dad is a captain in the Navy. He sails on the ocean in a large ship. Ann's dad is a pilot in the Air Force. He flies a jet. Juan and Ann miss their dads when they are gone for a long time. They write them letters and send them pictures. It is a happy day when their dads come home!

Draw a ☺ in the column under the correct dad.
Some sentences may describe both dads.

	Juan's dad	Ann's dad	Both dads
1. He is a captain.			
2. He works on a ship.			
3. Sometimes he is gone for a long time.			
4. He is a pilot.			
5. His child writes to him.			
6. He is in the Air Force.			
7. He is in the Navy.			
8. It is a happy time when he comes home.			
9. He flies a jet.			
10. He is a soldier.			

Scholastic

When you use your own thoughts to answer the question "How could that have happened?" you are **drawing conclusions**.

I bought a fancy rug today. It was made of brightly colored yarn. I placed it on the floor in front of the TV and sat on it. All of a sudden, it lifted me up in the air! The rug and I flew around the house. Then out the door we went. High above the trees, we soared like an eagle. Finally, the rug took me home, and we landed in my backyard.

How could that have happened? To find out, use your crayons to trace over each line. Use a different color on each line. Write the letter from that line in the box at the bottom of the rug.

Could this story really happen? Draw a rug around your answer.

Yes   **No**

Scholastic

Hello.

Hello, hello.

Have you ever heard a parrot talk? Parrots are able to copy sounds that they hear. You can train a parrot to repeat words, songs, and whistles. But a parrot cannot say words that it has never heard. People can use words to make new sentences, but most parrots cannot.

Read each sentence. If it is true, color the parrot under True. If it is false, color the parrot under False.

	True	False

1. You could teach a parrot to sing "Happy Birthday."

2. You could ask a parrot any question, and it could give the answer.

3. A parrot could make up a fairy tale.

4. If a parrot heard your mom say, "Brush your teeth," every night, he could learn to say it, too.

5. It is possible for a parrot to repeat words in Spanish.

Scholastic

When you use what you know to make a decision, you are making an inference. Use details from the story to make decisions about the characters.

Circle the picture that answers the riddle.

1. I have feathers. I also have wings, but I don't fly. I love to swim in icy water. Who am I?

2. I am 3 weeks old. I drink milk. I cry when my diaper is wet. Who am I?

3. I live in the ocean. I swim around slowly, looking for something to eat. I have six more arms than you have. Who am I?

4. I am an insect. If you touch me, I might bite you! I make tunnels under the ground. I love to come to your picnic! Who am I?

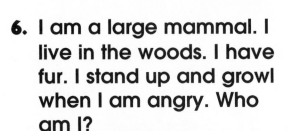

5. I am a female. I like to watch movies and listen to music. My grandchildren love my oatmeal cookies. Who am I?

6. I am a large mammal. I live in the woods. I have fur. I stand up and growl when I am angry. Who am I?

7. I wear a uniform. My job is to help people. I ride on a big red truck. Who am I?

Scholastic

Use story details to help you make decisions about the story.

James was the first boy in Miss Lane's class to sneeze. He sneezed and sneezed until his mom came to take him home. The next day, Amy and Jana started sneezing. The next Monday, six more children were absent. Finally, everyone got well and came back to school. But, this time Miss Lane was absent. Guess what was wrong with her!

Circle the correct answers.

1. **What do you think was wrong with the children?**

head cold   head lice   broken arms

2. **How do you know?**

The children sneezed.

The children came back to school.

3. **How many children in all got sick?**

4. **Why do you think Miss Lane was absent? Write your answer.**

_____

_____

Read the sentence below each picture. In the bubbles, write what each character could be saying.

Mr. Giraffe asked Mr. Zebra why he had stripes. Mr. Zebra didn't know.

Mr. Giraffe said that he should ask Mrs. Owl. Mr. Zebra agreed.

Mr. Zebra asked Mrs. Owl why he had stripes. Mrs. Owl laughed.

Mrs. Owl told Mr. Zebra that the Magic Fairy painted him that way!

Scholastic

*In a story, there is usually a reason something happens. This is the **cause**. What happens as a result is the **effect**.*

Sandy went on a vacation in the mountains with her parents and little brother Austin. They were staying in a small cabin without any electricity or running water. It was fun to have lanterns at night and to bathe in the cold mountain stream. The biggest problem for Sandy was she missed her best friend, Kendra. Sandy found her dad's cell phone and called Kendra. They talked for nearly an hour! When Sandy's dad went to call his office, the cell phone was dead. He was NOT a happy camper!

Draw a line to match the first part of each sentence to the second part that makes it true.

1. Sandy used lanterns at night because

2. Sandy bathed in a stream because

3. Sandy felt better about missing Kendra because

4. Sandy's dad could not call his office because

she talked to her on the cell phone.

the cabin had no running water.

the cabin had no electricity.

the cell phone was dead.

Scholastic

It is important to follow the rules at school. Read each rule below. Find the picture that shows what would happen if students DID NOT follow that rule. Write the letter of the picture in the correct box.

1. You must walk, not run, in the halls. ☐

2. Do not chew gum at school. ☐

3. Come to school on time. ☐

4. When the fire alarm rings, follow the leader outside. ☐

5. Listen when the teacher is talking. ☐

6. Keep your desk clean. ☐

*In a story, there is usually a reason something happens. This is the **cause**. What happens as a result is the **effect**.*

Wanda Wiggleworm was tired of living alone in the flowerpot, so she decided to live it up. Last night, Wanda went to the Ugly Bug Ball. She looked her best, all slick and slimy. Carl Caterpillar asked her to dance. They twisted and wiggled around and around to the music. All of a sudden, they got tangled up. They tried to get free, but instead, they tied themselves in a knot! What would they do? They decided to get married, and they lived happily ever after.

Unscramble each sentence about the story.
Write the new sentence on the line.

tangled	worms	when	got	danced.	they	The	up

_____

_____

in	knot	They	married.	a	they	were	so	got	tied

_____

_____

A character is a person or animal in a story. To help readers understand a character better, a story often gives details about the character.

Once upon a time there was a mixed-up queen named Margie. She got things mixed up. She wore her crown on her arm. She wore a shoe on her head. She painted every fingernail a different color. Then she painted her nose red! She used a fork to hold her hair in place. She wore a purple belt around her knees. The king didn't mind. He always wore his clothes backward!

Use the story and your crayons to help you follow these instructions:

1. Draw Margie's crown.

2. Draw her shoe.

3. Paint her fingernails and nose.

4. Draw what goes in her hair.

5. Draw her belt.

Circle the correct answer:

6. What makes you think Margie is mixed up?

    the way she dresses

    the way she talks

7. What makes you think the king is mixed up, too?

    He talks backward.

    He wears his clothes backward.

Scholastic

I love Miss Ticklefoot. She is my first-grade teacher.

To find out more about her, read each sentence below. Write a word in each blank that tells how she feels. The Word Box will help you.

Word Box

| sad | scared | silly | worried | happy | surprised |

1. Miss Ticklefoot smiles when we know the answers.

   _____

2. She is concerned when one of us is sick.

   _____

3. She makes funny faces at us during recess.

   _____

4. She cried when our fish died.

   _____

5. She jumps when the fire alarm rings.

   _____

6. Her mouth dropped open when we gave her a present!

   _____

Scholastic

When Ty was four years old, he had two make-believe friends named Mr. Go-Go and Mr. Sasso. They lived in Ty's closet. When there was no one else around, Ty talked to Mr. Go-Go while he played with his toys. Mr. Go-Go was a good friend. He helped put Ty's toys away. Mr. Sasso was not a good friend. Some days he forgot to make Ty's bed or brush Ty's teeth. One day he even talked back to Ty's mother. Another day Dad said, "Oh my! Who wrote on the wall?" Ty knew who did it . . . Mr. Sasso!

Read the phrase inside each crayon. If it describes Mr. Go-Go, color it green. If it describes Mr. Sasso, color it red. If it describes both, color it yellow.

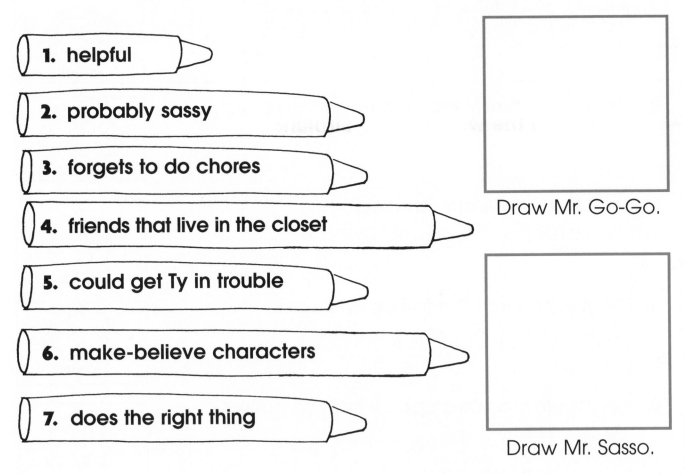

1. helpful

2. probably sassy

3. forgets to do chores

4. friends that live in the closet

5. could get Ty in trouble

6. make-believe characters

7. does the right thing

Draw Mr. Go-Go.

Draw Mr. Sasso.

Scholastic

Read the story then answer the questions.

My Uncle's Airplane

My uncle has a new airplane. It is yellow with blue stripes. The wings have stars on them. It flys high. He took me on a trip in his new plane. The name of his plane is Yellow Bird.

1. Who has a new airplane?

2. What are the colors of the airplane?

3. What are on the wings of the airplane?

4. Who took a trip in the new plane?

5. What is the name of the airplane?

6. Does the airplane fly high or low?

Read the story then answer the questions.

If I Were King

I would like to be a king. I would wear a robe with fur on it. I would wear a gold crown on my head. I would call the land I rule "Funville." Every year we would have a parade. I would want all of the people in Funville to be happy.

1. What would I like to be?

_____

2. What would be on my robe?

_____

3. What would I wear on my head?

_____

4. What would I call my land?

_____

5. What would happen every year in Funville?

_____

6. Do I want the people in Funville to be happy?

_____

Read the story then answer the questions.

Joel's Pets

Joel has three pets. He has two cats and one dog. Joel's cats are named Fifi and Foofoo. Joel's dog is named Hook. Joel gives his pets fresh food and water each day. He plays fetch with Hook.

1. How many pets does Joel have?

2. How many cats does Joel have?

3. How many dogs does Joel have?

4. What are the names of Joel's cats?

5. What is the name of Joel's dog?

6. What does Joel give to his pets?

Scholastic

Read the story then answer the questions.

Larry the Frog

Larry is a frog. Larry is green with brown spots. He loves to play in the pond. Sometimes Larry catches flies. He likes to eat flies for dinner. After Larry catches flies, he hops around the pond.

1. What is Larry?

_____

_____

2. What color is Larry?

_____

_____

3. Where does Larry love to play?

_____

_____

4. What does Larry catch?

_____

_____

5. What does Larry like to eat for dinner?

_____

_____

6. What does Larry do after he catches flies?

_____

_____

Scholastic

Read the story then answer the questions.

Karen's Doll

Karen's favorite toy is her doll. The doll's name is Kathy. Kathy has blond hair and wears a pink dress. Karen was three years old when she got her doll. Kathy sleeps on Karen's bed when Karen is at school.

1. What is Karen's favorite toy?

- -

2. What is the name of Karen's doll?

- -

3. What color is Kathy's hair?

- -

4. What color is Kathy's dress?

- -

5. What does Kathy do when Karen is at school?

- -

6. Is Kathy a real person?

- -

Read the story then answer the questions.

Chris Likes Science

My name is Chris. I like to read. I like stories about stars and planets the best. The book I am reading now is about the sun. The book has many pictures. It has a picture of the sun on the cover. We will study the sun in science class next year.

1. What is my name?

_____

- -

_____

2. What kind of books do I like?

_____

- -

_____

3. What am I reading about now?

_____

- -

_____

4. What does the book I am reading have a lot of?

_____

- -

_____

5. What is on the cover of this book?

_____

- -

_____

6. What will I study next year at school?

_____

- -

_____

Read the story then answer the questions.

Rainy Day

Roy likes to play in the rain. When it rains, he puts on his raincoat and boots. He goes outside. Roy splashes in the puddles. Roy must think that he is a duck. Sometimes Meyer plays in the rain with Roy.

1. What does Roy like to play in?

----

2. What does Roy put on when it rains?

----

3. Where does Roy go?

----

4. What does Roy splash in?

----

5. What must Roy think he is?

----

6. Who plays in the rain with Roy sometimes?

Read the story then answer the questions.

Rowe's Dog

My friend Rowe has a dog. I really like Rowe's dog. His dog is brown. She wears a red collar. Rowe plays with the dog a lot. Rowe's dog loves to chew on bones. I wish I had a dog like Rowe's.

1. What does my friend Rowe have?

_____

_____

2. **Do I like Rowe's dog?**

_____

_____

3. What color is Rowe's dog?

_____

_____

4. What color is the dog's collar?

_____

_____

5. What does Rowe's dog chew on?

_____

_____

6. What do I wish?

_____

_____

Scholastic

Read the story then answer the questions.

Baby Chickens

A mother chicken sat on her nest. She was a big chicken with yellow feathers. She was sitting on some eggs. One day the eggs cracked open. Then some little chicks popped out of the eggs. Now the chicken had six chicks.

1. Where did the mother chicken sit?

_____

_____

2. What color were her feathers?

_____

_____

3. What was the mother chicken sitting on?

_____

_____

4. What happened to the eggs one day?

_____

_____

5. What came out of the eggs?

_____

_____

6. How many chicks were there?

_____

_____

Scholastic

Read the story then answer the questions.

Wally the Whale

Wally is a big blue whale. Wally lives in the ocean. He swims with his whale friends. Sometimes Wally dives deep then he jumps high into the air. When he lands in the water, Wally makes a big splash.

1. What kind of animal is Wally?

_____

- -

_____

2. What color is Wally?

_____

- -

_____

3. Where does Wally live?

_____

- -

_____

4. Who does Wally swim with?

_____

- -

_____

5. What does Wally do after he dives deep?

_____

- -

_____

6. What happens when Wally lands in the water?

_____

- -

_____

Reading Skills & Reading Comprehension Practice Test

Fill in the bubble next to the sentence that tells about each picture.

Example

- ● **A** A girl sits.
- ○ **B** A girl walks.
- ○ **C** A girl runs.
- ○ **D** A girl eats.

1.

- ○ **A** The boy plays ball.
- ○ **B** The cat plays.
- ○ **C** The girls run and play.
- ○ **D** The cat runs.

2.

- ○ **F** The book is on the desk.
- ○ **G** He has two books.
- ○ **H** The pen is next to the book.
- ○ **J** The book is on the chair.

3.

- ○ **A** We have a big bag.
- ○ **B** She has a rabbit.
- ○ **C** He has a rug and a pan.
- ○ **D** She has a cat.

4.

- ○ **F** Six pigs sit.
- ○ **G** The dog sits on a hill.
- ○ **H** A pig plays in the mud.
- ○ **J** A cat climbs a tree.

Reading Skills & Reading Comprehension Practice Test

Read the story then answer each question. Fill in the bubble next to the best answer.

> Pam has a dog. His name is Rags.
> Rags likes to play.
> Rags likes to run.
> Rags likes to jump.
> Rags is a good dog!

1. What kind of pet does Pam have?

- ○ **A**   cat
- ○ **B**   dog
- ○ **C**   rabbit
- ○ **D**   gerbil

2. What is a good title (name) for this story?

- ○ **F**   Rags the Dog
- ○ **G**   Frogs Jump
- ○ **H**   Apples Grow on Trees
- ○ **J**   Pam has a Bad Dog

3. What does Rags like to do?

- ○ **A**   skip
- ○ **B**   play
- ○ **C**   sing
- ○ **D**   eat

Scholastic

Reading Skills & Reading Comprehension Practice Test

Fill in the bubble next to the correct answer.

1. What letter is in PAT, but not CAT?

○ **A**   P
○ **B**   C
○ **C**   A
○ **D**   T

2. Fill in the bubble next to the event that comes first.

○ **F**   Sue eats a piece of cake.
○ **G**   Mom opens the cake mix.
○ **H**   Sue adds eggs and milk to the mix.
○ **J**   Mom puts the mix in a bowl.

3. Fill in the bubble that answers the riddle.

I am an insect.

I bite people.

People don't like me.

I leave red marks on people.

Who am I?

○ **A**   a slug
○ **B**   a mosquito
○ **C**   a ladybug
○ **D**   a grasshopper

Scholastic

Reading Skills & Reading Comprehension Practice Test

Choose a sticker to place here.

Fill in the bubble next to the correct answer.

4. Which of the following does not belong in a group labeled food?

    ◯ **A**   spinach

    ◯ **B**   bread

    ◯ **C**   napkin

    ◯ **D**   milk

5. Carl missed the school bus. Fill in the bubble next to the answer that tells why.

    ◯ **F**   Carl was waiting for the bus.

    ◯ **G**   Carl did not have school that day.

    ◯ **H**   Carl met his friend.

    ◯ **J**   Carl got out of bed late.

6. Maria is a character in a story. She has lots of friends. Maria is kind and helpful. Which word below best describes her.

    ◯ **A**   mean

    ◯ **B**   pretty

    ◯ **C**   nice

    ◯ **D**   silly

Scholastic

Vocabulary

Your child is introduced to a variety of words in this section. Building a strong vocabulary is an important step in becoming a strong reader.

What to Do

Have your child work on the activity pages. Review his or her work. Ask your child if he or she has learned new words. Encourage your child to add them to the Master Word List. Review the words on the list periodically.

Paste the flash cards on pages 159–164 onto cardboard or poster board. Then cut them out. Use them to build and reinforce vocabulary development.

Keep On Going!

Play a word game with your child. Say a word and ask your child to tell you an antonym (opposite) and a synonym (same meaning) for the word.

antonym

Synonym

Synonyms *are words with the same or nearly the same meanings.*

Read each word at the top of the box. Circle every other letter. Write the letters in order on the line to spell a synonym. The first one is done for you.

1. begin

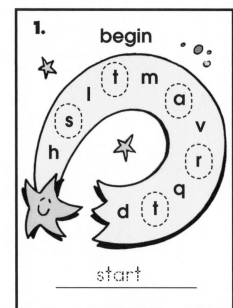

start

2. glad

3. loud

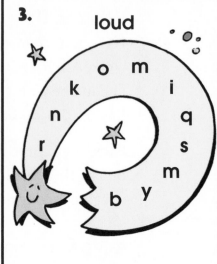

4. little

5. see

6. big

Scholastic

Antonyms *are words with opposite meanings.*

Read the word on each flowerpot. Color the flower with the antonym.

Compound words *are two words joined together to make a new word.*

Draw a line to connect the boxes to make compound words.
Write the compound word.

door		hive		1. _____
foot		flower		2. _____
sun		time		3. _____
cup		bell		4. _____
bee		brush		5. _____
bed		ball		6. _____
flower		shelf		7. _____
dog		cake		8. _____
pop		corn		9. _____
tooth		pot		10. _____
book		house		11. _____

Scholastic

Homophones *are words that sound alike but are spelled differently and have different meanings.*

a	b	c	d	e	g	h	i	k	l	m	n	o	r	s	t	u	w	y
☺	🕐	⇨	☆	★	⧗	❀	✋	✗	✓	◐	❋	⚓	□	◆	❄	◆	🗴	◈

Use the code to write each homophone.

1. here   ___ ___ ___ ___

2. know   ___ ___

3. to   ___ ___ ___

4. ate   ___ ___ ___ ___ ___

5. cent   ___ ___ ___ ___ ___

6. break   ___ ___ ___ ___ ___

7. so   ___ ___ ___

8. main   ___ ___ ___ ___
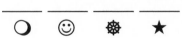

9. road   ___ ___ ___ ___
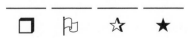

Unscramble the shape words. Write the words on the lines.

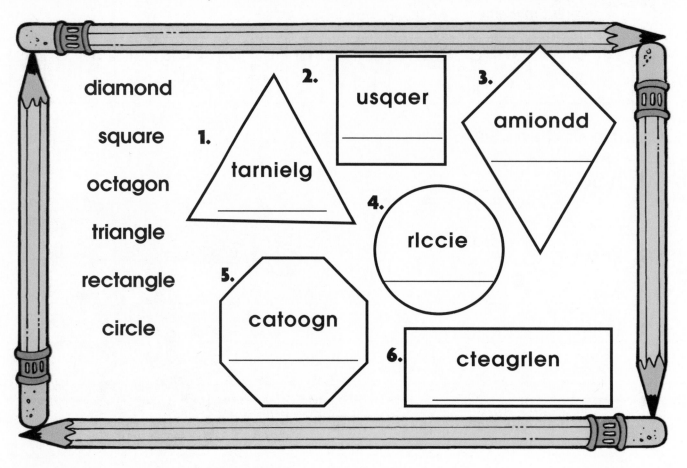

diamond

square

octagon

triangle

rectangle

circle

1. tarnielg _____

2. usqaer _____

3. amiondd _____

4. rlccie _____

5. catoogn _____

6. cteagrlen _____

What shape is a . . .

7. pizza? _____

8. ball infield? _____

9. tent? _____

10. sign? _____

11. present? _____

12. window? _____

 Find eight things in your home that are shaped like a rectangle. Name them.

Scholastic

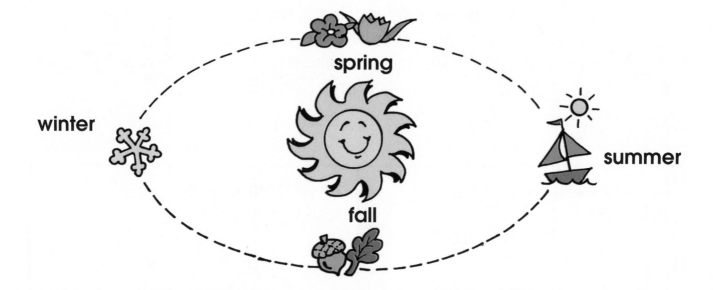

Circle the season that goes with each sentence.

1. Birds make nests for babies.

2. Children build snowmen.

3. Leaves turn red, orange, and yellow.

4. Children go swimming outside.

5. Flowers begin to bloom.

6. Some animals hibernate.

7. Trees start losing leaves.

8. Insects fly through the air.

Look at the weather picture. Read the weather clue. Cross out every other letter box. The letters left will name the kind of weather. Write the weather word on the line. The first one has been done for you.

I see nothing but snow.

| b | ~~e~~ | l | ~~i~~ | s | ~~z~~ | a | ~~z~~ | i | ~~a~~ | o | ~~r~~ | f | ~~d~~ |

1. _____blizzard_____

I see balls of ice falling from the sky.

| h | j | a | j | i | q | l |

2. _____

I see a dark funnel cloud in the sky.

| t | r | o | p | r | b | n | g | a | j | d | u | o |

3. _____

I see water drops falling from the sky.

| r | g | a | k | i | a | n |

4. _____

I see white flakes falling from the sky.

| s | e | n | b | o | i | w |

5. _____

I see beautiful blue skies.

| s | f | u | s | n | c | s | l | h | o | i | r | n | r | e |

6. _____

Scholastic

Read each clue. Write the names of the correct animals in the crossword puzzle.

Across

2. This mammal hibernates in the winter.

5. This reptile has a long nose and sharp teeth.

6. This mammal makes an oink sound.

7. This mammal has a mane.

Down

1. This bird uses its wings to swim.

3. This mammal lives like a fish.

4. This sea creature has eight arms.

Cross out every other letter to name the baby animal. Write the name on the line. The first one has been done for you.

k ~~j~~ i ~~u~~ t ~~g~~ t ~~b~~ e ~~s~~ n	l v a g m c b
kitten	
1._____	2._____

t h a t d a p k o r l f e	d f u j c w k d l n i k n o g
3._____	4._____

f c a i w d n	c e u x b
5._____	6._____

c l a d l n f	p d i h g y l i e b t
7._____	8._____

c o h r i e c q k	p b u u p a p z y
9._____	10._____

Read each clue. Write the name of each community helper.

1. I give you a checkup
each year as you grow up.

___ ___ ___ ___ ___ ___
　5

2. I drive a vehicle that is really cool.
I pick you up each day for school.

___ ___ ___ ___ ___ ___ ___ ___ ___ ___
　　6

3. When smoke hits your nose
I'll come with my hose.

___ ___ ___ ___ ___ ___ ___ ___ ___ ___ ___
　　　　　2

4. I work on your teeth awhile, so
you can have a bright smile.

___ ___ ___ ___ ___ ___ ___
　　　4

5. I share a lot for you to learn,
and in my class we all take turns.

___ ___ ___ ___ ___ ___ ___
　1

6. I am here to help you look
for an interesting book.

___ ___ ___ ___ ___ ___ ___ ___ ___
　　　　　　　3

Use the letters from above to finish the sentence.

For all you do, we say . . .

___ ___ ___ ___k　y ___ ___!
　1　 2　 3　 4　　　 5　 6

bus driver　　　　doctor　　　　dentist

librarian　　　　firefighter　　　　teacher

Scholastic

Circle the transportation words in the letter grid. The words go across and down.

airplane

sailboat

van

bus

ship

canoe

train

helicopter

truck

car

bike

s	h	i	p	a	n	a
a	e	t	d	o	b	i
i	l	s	v	a	i	r
l	i	t	a	k	k	p
b	c	a	n	o	e	l
o	o	e	r	c	f	a
a	p	u	c	a	r	n
t	t	r	u	c	k	e
r	e	v	h	b	u	s
t	r	a	i	n	l	s

Complete the chart to identify different kinds of transportation.

air	land	water
_____	_____	_____
_____	_____	_____
	_____	_____
	_____	
	_____	
	_____	

Use the code to fill in the blanks about parts of a map.

a	b	c	e	h	k	l	m	n	o	p	r	s	t	u	w	y
↖	✴	○	❋	◆	✪	✧	☑	➴	✿	❀	♩	◁	⊙	◷	☺	↗

1. A map __ __ __ __ __ __ is a
   ◁ ↗ ☑ ✴ ✿ ✧

   picture that stands for a real thing.

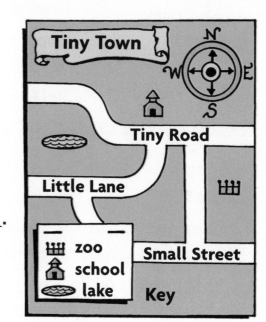

2. A list of symbols and what they stand

   for is called the __ __ __ __ __ __.
   ☑ ↖ ❀ ✪ ❋ ↗

3. The cardinal directions are

   __ __ __ __ __, __ __ __ __ __,
   ➴ ✿ ♩ ⊙ ◆   ◁ ✿ ◷ ⊙ ◆

   __ __ __ __, and __ __ __ __.
   ❋ ↖ ◁ ⊙   ☺ ❋ ◁ ⊙

4. The __ __ __ __ __ __ __ __ __ __ __
      ○ ✿ ☑ ❀ ↖ ◁ ◁   ♩ ✿ ◁ ❋

   shows the cardinal directions on a map.

Use the map to complete the crossword puzzle.

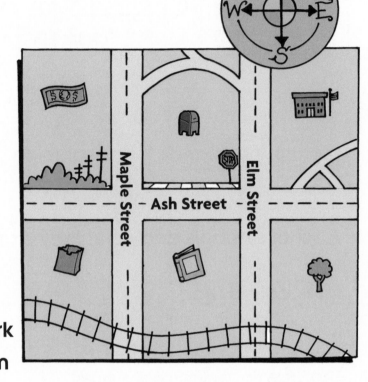

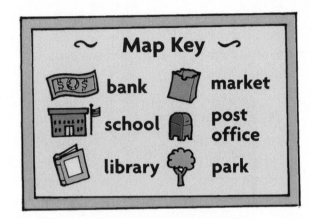

Across

3. the first street crossed if walking west from the park

5. the direction to travel from the market to the bank

6. the direction to travel from the post office to the school

| north | south | east | west |

Down

1. the direction to travel from the library to the market

2. the first street crossed if walking east from the bank

4. the direction to travel from the school to the park

7. the street crossed if walking north from the library

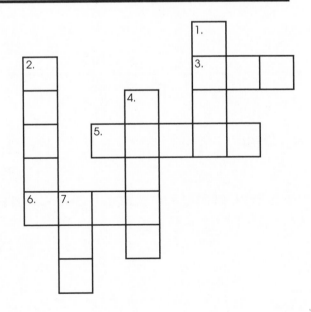

Scholastic

Use a word from the box to describe the character trait shown in each picture.

| polite | cooperative | helpful | honest | responsible | kind |

1. _____

2. _____

3. _____

4. _____

5. _____

6. _____

*An **analogy** is a comparison between two things that are similar in some respects.*

Finish each analogy using the Word Bank. Write the word on the line.

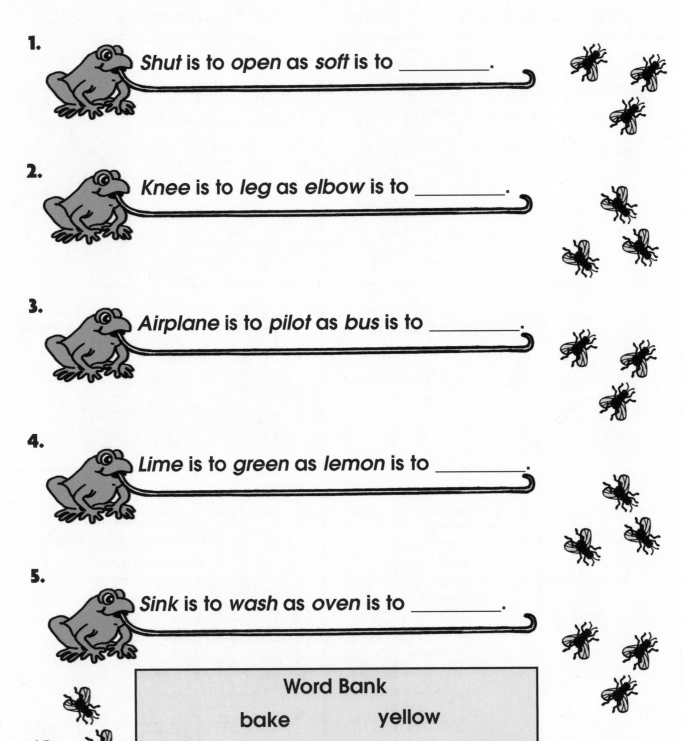

1. **Shut** is to **open** as **soft** is to _____.

2. **Knee** is to **leg** as **elbow** is to _____.

3. **Airplane** is to **pilot** as **bus** is to _____.

4. **Lime** is to **green** as **lemon** is to _____.

5. **Sink** is to **wash** as **oven** is to _____.

Word Bank

bake   yellow

hard   arm   driver

Scholastic

Complete each analogy using a word from the box. Color each word to show the path through the maze.

1. *Knife* is to *cut* as *pencil* is to _____.

2. *Pig* is to *squeal* as *dog* is to _____.

3. *Finger* is to *hand* as *toe* is to _____.

4. *Tall* is to *short* as *high* is to _____.

5. *Animal* is to *zoo* as *clown* is to _____.

6. *Wing* is to *bird* as *fin* is to _____.

7. *Juice* is to *drink* as *steak* is to _____.

8. *Cat* is to *meow* as *lion* is to _____.

9. *Smile* is to *frown* as *up* is to _____.

foot	fish	boy	fly	cook
hand	write	under	pet	sleep
elbow	bark	laugh	read	cut
flower	low	play	arm	knee
movie	roar	circus	eat	down

Write the missing word to complete each analogy. Color the words below to help the elephant get to the camel.

1. *Knife* is to *cut* as *broom* is to _____.

2. *Early* is to *late* as *light* is to _____.

3. *Short* is to *tall* as *small* is to _____.

4. *Question* is to *answer* as *empty* is to _____.

5. *Quiet* is to *noisy* as *hot* is to _____.

6. *Shout* is to *whisper* as *wide* is to _____.

7. *Empty* is to *full* as *clean* is to _____.

8. *Boat* is to *water* as *plane* is to _____.

9. *In* is to *out* as *happy* is to _____.

10. *Elephant* is to *trunk* as *camel* is to _____.

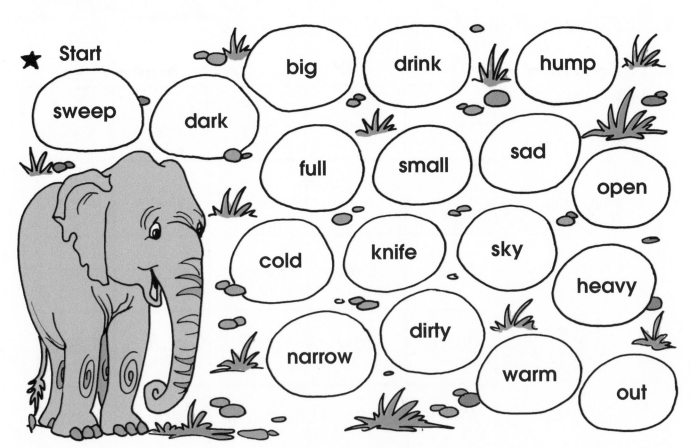

★ Start

sweep   dark   big   drink   hump

full   small   sad   open

cold   knife   sky   heavy

narrow   dirty   warm   out

Scholastic

begin	see
start	look
glad	big
happy	large
loud	down
noisy	up
little	under
small	over

diamond	fall
square	summer
octagon	blizzard
triangle	rain
rectangle	snow
circle	sunshine
winter	cloud
spring	sky

bus driver	car
doctor	bike
dentist	truck
firefighter	train
teacher	north
airplane	south
bus	east
ship	west

Vocabulary Practice Test

Fill in the bubble next to the correct answer.

1. Which word means the same as big?
   ○ **A** tiny
   ○ **B** large
   ○ **C** small
   ○ **D** lean

2. Which word has the opposite meaning to cold?
   ○ **F** chilly
   ○ **G** freezing
   ○ **H** cool
   ○ **J** hot

3. Which word is a homophone of write?
   ○ **A** weight
   ○ **B** right
   ○ **C** wait
   ○ **D** waste

Vocabulary Practice Test

Fill in the bubble next to the correct answer.

4. Which season has the hottest weather?

○ **A** summer

○ **B** winter

○ **C** spring

○ **D** fall

5. Which weather word describes water falling from the sky?

○ **F** snow

○ **G** rain

○ **H** hail

○ **J** blizzard

6. Which word is the name for a bear's baby?

○ **A** kitten

○ **B** cub

○ **C** calf

○ **D** puppy

Vocabulary Practice Test

Fill in the bubble next to the correct answer.

7. Which community helper will help you find a good book to read?

○ **A**   librarian

○ **B**   police officer

○ **C**   firefighter

○ **D**   dentist

8. Which part of a map has a list of symbols and what they stand for?

○ **F**   compass

○ **G**   title

○ **H**   key

○ **J**   scale

9. Which word is a direction word?

○ **A**   very

○ **B**   big

○ **C**   north

○ **D**   happy

Vocabulary Practice Test

Fill in the bubble next to the correct answer.

10. Which word describes a shape with three sides?

○ **A**   square

○ **B**   circle

○ **C**   triangle

○ **D**   diamond

11. Which animal lives in the ocean?

○ **F**   octopus

○ **G**   pig

○ **H**   lion

○ **J**   bear

12. Which word completes the analogy?

Big is to **large** as **tiny** is to _____.

○ **A**   round

○ **B**   huge

○ **C**   full

○ **D**   little

Scholastic

Grammar/Writing

To be successful at playing a game, you have to understand the rules. The same thing is true of writing. Grammar provides the rules your child will use to become a successful writer.

In this section, your child will learn the parts of speech: nouns, pronouns, verbs, adverbs, and adjectives. He or she will also learn three types of sentences—declarative, interrogative, and exclamatory—and how each is punctuated.

What to Do
Have your child complete the activities on each page. Review the answers together.

Keep On Going!
Play a grammar/spelling riddle game with your child. Make up riddles for your child to solve such as:

> We are describing words.
> You might use us to describe a friend.
> What words might we be? (*kind, nice*)
>
> Write a sentence using those words.

Take turns and have your child make up riddles for you to guess.

noun

verb

adjective

*A sentence begins with a **capital letter**.*

Help the mouse get to the cheese by coloring each box with a word that begins with a capital letter.

The	For	That	with	know	but
here	on	When	Have	next	we
as	after	good	Make	there	see
Go	Look	Are	Could	is	why
This	who	said	in	come	them
Has	Name	Before	Her	Where	The

Scholastic

*A sentence always begins with a **capital letter**.*

Copy each sentence correctly on the line.

1 the cat sat.

_____

- -

_____

2 the dog sat.

_____

- -

_____

3 i see the cat.

_____

- -

_____

4 i can see.

_____

- -

_____

Scholastic

*A telling sentence ends with a **period**.*

Write a period where it belongs in each sentence. Read the
sentences to a friend.

1 **Dan is in the cab**

2 **The cat is in the cab**

3 **Mom is in the cab**

4 **We see Dan and Mom**

Read the words. Write each word and period at the end
of the correct sentence.

van.　　red.

5 **We can go in the** _____

6 **The van is** _____

Scholastic

*A sentence has a **naming part**. It tells who or what the sentence is about.*

Color the snake that tells the naming part in each sentence below.

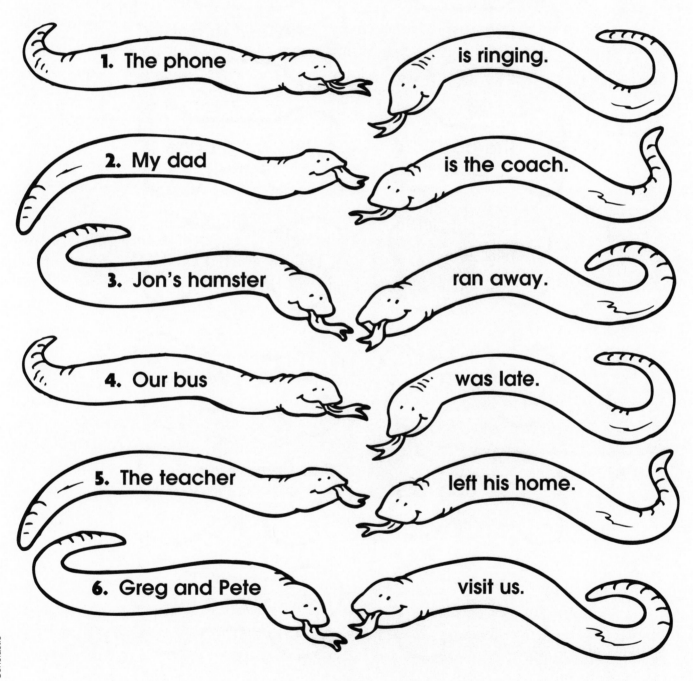

1. The phone   is ringing.

2. My dad   is the coach.

3. Jon's hamster   ran away.

4. Our bus   was late.

5. The teacher   left his home.

6. Greg and Pete   visit us.

Scholastic

*A sentence has an **action part**. It tells what is happening.*

Color the bone that tells the action part in each sentence below.

1. The dog   chases the cat.

2. The dog   hides the bone.

3. The dog   plays with a ball.

4. The dog   jumps in the air.

5. The dog   eats a bone.

6. The dog   sleeps on a rug.

Scholastic

Color each flag that tells a complete thought. Leave the other
flags blank.

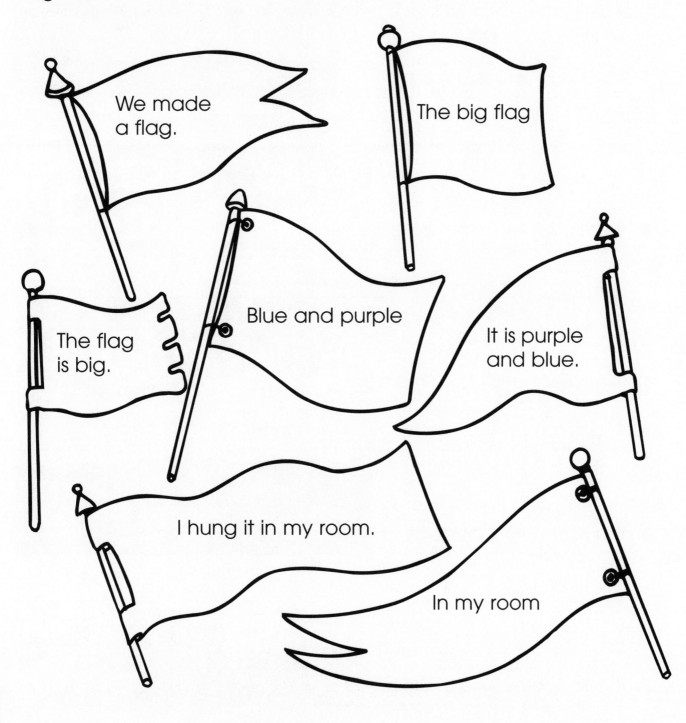

Scholastic

A **telling sentence** *begins with a* **capital letter** *and ends with a* **period**.

Rewrite each sentence correctly.

1. frogs and toads lay eggs

_____

_____

2. the eggs are in the water

_____

_____

3. tadpoles hatch from the eggs

_____

_____

4. the tadpoles grow legs

_____

_____

5. the tadpoles lose their tails

_____

_____

Scholastic

Question sentences *ask something. They end with a* **question mark** *(?).*

Read each sentence. Circle each question mark.

1 **Who hid the hat?**

2 **Is it on the cat?**

3 **Can you see the hat?**

4 **Is it on the man?**

Write two questions. Draw a line under the capital letter at the beginning of each question. Circle the question marks.

5 _____

6 _____

➤ **Exclamatory sentences** *show strong feeling, such as excitement, surprise, or fear. They end with an* **exclamation mark** *(!).*

Choose the sentence in each pair that shows strong feeling. Write it on the line. Put an exclamation mark at the end.

1 Run to the show   We will go to the show

_____

2 I'm late for it   Oh my, I'm very late

_____

3 What a great show   I liked the show

_____

4 The floor is wet   Watch out, the floor is wet

_____

5 We had fun   Wow, we had lots of fun

_____

Scholastic

Words in a sentence must be in an order that makes sense.

Read each group of words. Write them in the right order on the lines.

1

_____

- -

_____

2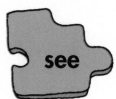

_____

- -

_____

3

_____

- -

_____

Words in a sentence must be in an order that makes sense.

These words are mixed up. Put them in order.
Then write each sentence.

1   snow.   bear   likes   This

_____

- -

_____

2   water   cold.   The   is

_____

- -

_____

3   fast.   The   runs   bear

_____

- -

_____

4   play.   bears   Two

_____

- -

_____

Scholastic

*Always write the word **I** with a capital letter.*

Read the sentences. Write **I** on the line.

1 _____ will ride.

2 _____ will swim.

3 Mom and _____ will sing.

4 Then _____ will read.

What will you do next? Write it on the line.

5 I will

Scholastic

The names of people, places, and pets are special. They begin with capital letters.

Circle each special name. Draw a line under the capital letter in each name.

1 I am Pam.

2 I sit on Ant Hill.

3 Ron likes the lake.

4 He likes Bat Lake.

Read the special names in the box.
Write a special name for each picture.

Spot   Hill Street

5

6

Scholastic

*A **noun** is a naming word. It names a person, place, or thing.*

Read each sentence. Circle each noun. Draw a line to match the sentence to the picture of the naming word.

1 **Run and kick in the park.**

2 **Kick with a foot.**

3 **Kick the ball.**

4 **The girl will run to get it.**

5 **Kick it to the net.**

Scholastic

Read each sentence. Fill in the circle next to the word that names a person, place, or thing.

1 **Let's play in the park.**

   ○ **A**   play

   ○ **B**   Let's

   ○ **C**   park

   ○ **D**   the

2 **The girl can run and kick.**

   ○ **F**   girl

   ○ **G**   run

   ○ **H**   kick

   ○ **J**   and

3 **Kick the ball hard.**

   ○ **A**   ball

   ○ **B**   the

   ○ **C**   kick

   ○ **D**   hard

4 **The friend can jump.**

   ○ **F**   can

   ○ **G**   jump

   ○ **H**   friend

   ○ **J**   the

5 **Jump to the net.**

   ○ **A**   get

   ○ **B**   net

   ○ **C**   jump

   ○ **D**   do

Scholastic

*Many nouns, or naming words, add **-s** to show more than one.*

Read the sets of sentences. Draw a line under the sentence that has a naming word that names more than one.

1 Jan has her mittens.

Jan has her mitten.

2 She will run up a hill.

She will run up hills.

3 Jan runs with her dogs.

Jan runs with her dog.

4 The dogs can jump.

The dog can jump.

Look at each picture. Read each word. Write the plural naming word that matches the picture.

5

cat _____

6

sock _____

A **verb** is an action word. It tells what happens.

Look at each picture. Read the words. Write the action word.

1 **Ann sees.**

_____
- - - - - - - - - - - - - - -
_____

2  **The cat sits.**

_____
- - - - - - - - - - - - - - -
_____

3  **Mom mops.**

_____
- - - - - - - - - - - - - - -
_____

4  **We run fast.**

_____
- - - - - - - - - - - - - - -
_____

5  **It hops a lot.**

Is, are, was, *and* **were** *are* **linking verbs. Is** *tells about one.* **Are** *tells about more than one.* **Was** *tells about one in the past.* **Were** *tells about more than one in the past.*

Circle the linking verb. Write **now** or **past** to tell when the action happens or happened.

1 The chicks are eating. _____

2 The duck is swimming. _____

3 The cat was napping. _____

4 The pig is digging. _____

5 They were playing. _____

Fill in the oval next to the linking verb that completes each sentence.

1 **The hen ___ sitting.**

- ⬭ **was**
- ⬭ **are**
- ⬭ **were**

2 **They ___ playing.**

- ⬭ **were**
- ⬭ **is**
- ⬭ **was**

3 **The pigs ___ digging.**

- ⬭ **was**
- ⬭ **is**
- ⬭ **are**

4 **The duck ___ swimming.**

- ⬭ **were**
- ⬭ **is**
- ⬭ **are**

5 **The chicks ___ napping.**

- ⬭ **was**
- ⬭ **is**
- ⬭ **are**

Scholastic

*Add **-ed** to most verbs, or action words, to tell about the past.*

A. Read each sentence. Circle the verb that tells about the past.

1. He looked at the dinosaur.

2. He talked to the dinosaur.

3. He waved to the dinosaur.

4. He smiled at the dinosaur.

5. She played with the dinosaur.

B. Circle the verbs that tell about the past. Use one to write a sentence about a dinosaur.

play	played	walk	walked	jump	jumped

_____

_____

_____

_____

Scholastic

*Add **-ed** to most verbs, or action words, to tell about the past.*

A. Read each sentence and the two verbs. Write the past-tense verb in the sentence.

1. The children _____ the fish. (love/loved)

2. They _____ to see more fish. (ask/asked)

3. The fish _____ up to see them. (jump/jumped)

B. Write a verb from the box. Then add an ending to make the verb tell about the past.

wave	talk	walk	jump	ask

_____

- -

_____

Describing words *help you imagine how something looks, feels, smells, sounds, or tastes.*

Read the describing words to guess the mystery object. Use the Word Bank to help you.

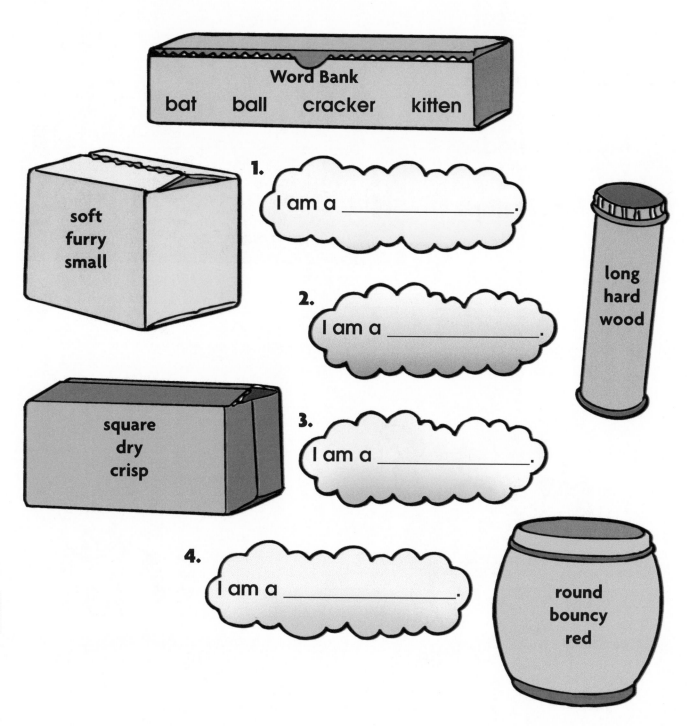

Word Bank

bat   ball   cracker   kitten

soft
furry
small

1. I am a _____.

2. I am a _____.

long
hard
wood

square
dry
crisp

3. I am a _____.

4. I am a _____.

round
bouncy
red

Scholastic

An **adjective** *is a* **describing word**. *It tells more about a person, place, or thing.*

Read each sentence. Circle the
word that tells about the cat.

1 I see a **big** cat.

2 The **fast** cat ran.

3 My cat is **bad**.

4 The **fat** cat naps.

Look at each cat. Circle the word that tells about it.

5 **fat**   **little**

6 **big**   **little**

Scholastic

*The **describing words** in a sentence help the reader paint a picture in his or her mind.*

Write three words to describe each gift. Then color them to match.

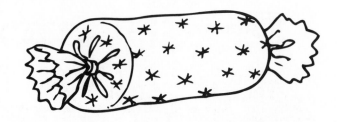

1. _____ (color)

_____ (color)

_____ (pattern)

2. _____ (color)

_____ (color)

_____ (pattern)

3. _____ (color)

_____ (color)

_____ (pattern)

4. _____ (color)

_____ (color)

_____ (pattern)

*A sentence is more interesting when it tells **where** the action is happening.*

Write an ending for each sentence that tells **where** the action takes place.

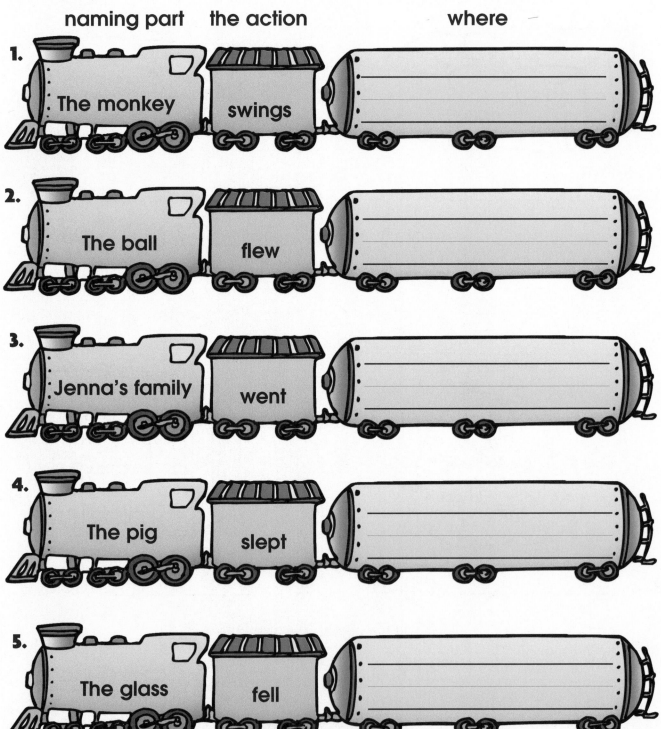

naming part   the action   where

1. The monkey   swings

2. The ball   flew

3. Jenna's family   went

4. The pig   slept

5. The glass   fell

Scholastic

*A sentence may also tell **when** the action takes place.*

Circle the part that tells when in each sentence.

1. George Washington lived long ago.

2. The mail carrier was late yesterday.

3. The bear slept in winter.

4. We are going to the zoo today.

5. The leaves change in the fall.

6. I lost my tooth last night.

7. It rained all day.

8. The party starts at noon.

9. We got home yesterday.

10. We ate turkey on Thanksgiving Day.

11. The kitten was playing this morning.

12. Tomorrow I am going to my grandmother's house.

Scholastic

Use choices from each part to make three "sweet" sentences.

naming part	action	where or when
I	ate doughnuts	at the bakery.
She	ate candy	at the party.
He	chewed gum	at the circus.

1.

2.

3.

Scholastic

Sentences can be written in order to give directions.

Finish each set of directions by writing sentences about the last two pictures.

1. **First,** <u>mix all the ingredients.</u>

Next, _____

_____

Last, _____

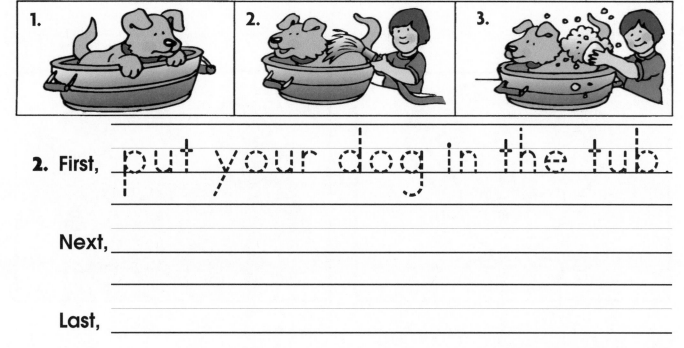

2. **First,** <u>put your dog in the tub</u>

Next, _____

_____

Last, _____

*The name of a story is called the **title**. It matches with the story. Most of the words in a title begin with capital letters.*

Match each title with its story. Write the title above the picture.

A Big Beak	The Big Win
My Space Friend	A Knight's Tale

1. _____
(title)

2. _____
(title)

3. _____
(title)

4. _____
(title)

Scholastic

*Words that compare two people, places, or things end in **-er**.*

Read each sentence. Circle the word that compares. Then draw a line under the two words that name the two things that are being compared.

1. Beth is older than Carmen.

2. The tree is taller than the bush.

3. The plant is smaller than the tree.

4. The fly is faster than the ant.

Read each word. Then write the comparing word.

5. tall _____

6. old _____

7. slow _____

8. bold _____

Scholastic

He, she, they, we, *and* **I** *are subject pronouns. They can take the place of nouns, or naming words.*

Read each sentence pair. Circle the subject pronoun. Draw a line under the naming word or words it takes the place of.

1. Kim was bored. She went to the market.

2. Kim met Jo. They looked around the market.

3. Jo got bored. He went home.

4. Kim bought a mango. It tasted very sweet.

5. Then Kim became tired. She went home.

Read the sentence. Write it again, but replace a pronoun for the underlined words.

6. <u>The people</u> looked for mangoes.

_____

- -

_____

_____

- -

_____

Scholastic

He, she, they, we, *and* **I** *are subject pronouns. They can take the place of nouns, or naming words.*

Read each set of sentences and the underlined naming word or words. Then circle the pronoun.

1. <u>Mama</u> is happy. She smiles.

2. <u>The market</u> is fun. It is busy.

3. <u>Yemi</u> is sad. She looks for Kokou.

4. <u>Kokou</u> is little. He is a baby.

5. <u>Steven</u> is kind. He is my friend.

6. <u>Carlos</u> and <u>Tony</u> are in the same class. They are friends.

7. <u>Patti</u> and I like to act. We are in the school play.

Scholastic

Grammar/Writing Practice Test

Fill in the bubble next to the correct answer.

1. Which name is written correctly?

   ○ **A**   kim

   ○ **B**   Mike

   ○ **C**   ted

   ○ **D**   troy

2. Which sentence is written correctly?

   ○ **F**   they went to the movies

   ○ **G**   Emilio is my best friend

   ○ **H**   She lives in the green house.

   ○ **J**   I love to play soccer

3. Which sentence is a telling sentence?

   ○ **A**   Do you have my pen?

   ○ **B**   Where is your dog?

   ○ **C**   I want to go swimming.

   ○ **D**   Be careful!

Scholastic

Grammar/Writing Practice Test

Fill in the bubble next to the correct answer.

4. Which word is an action verb?

◯ **A**   runs

◯ **B**   under

◯ **C**   is

◯ **D**   sun

5. Which word is a proper noun?

◯ **F**   tree

◯ **G**   Bea

◯ **H**   bee

◯ **J**   flower

6. Which word might you use to describe your pet rabbit?

◯ **A**   furry

◯ **B**   flight

◯ **C**   feed

◯ **D**   feel

Grammar/Writing Practice Test

Fill in the bubble next to the correct answer.

7. Which pronoun would you use to replace Ben?

   ◯ **A**   I

   ◯ **B**   she

   ◯ **C**   they

   ◯ **D**   he

8. Which sentence shows strong feeling?

   ◯ **F**   Is that a banana?

   ◯ **G**   Come over for dinner.

   ◯ **H**   This pie tastes great!

   ◯ **J**   I am tired.

9. Which sentence has a past-tense verb?

   ◯ **A**   We are going to the zoo.

   ◯ **B**   I am very hungry.

   ◯ **C**   He walked all the way home.

   ◯ **D**   My teacher talks a lot.

Grammar/Writing Practice Test

Fill in the bubble next to the correct answer.

10. Which word in the following sentence is a describing word?

She found a yellow hat in the closet.

○ **A** yellow

○ **B** found

○ **C** hat

○ **D** closet

11. Which word in the sentence tells where something happened?

The baby birds stayed inside.

○ **F** baby

○ **G** birds

○ **H** stayed

○ **J** inside

12. Which word compares two things?

○ **A** small

○ **B** little

○ **C** smaller

○ **D** tiny

Scholastic

Addition

In this section, your child will practice basic addition facts. He or she will learn to add single and double-digit numbers without regrouping.

What to Do
Have your child complete the problems on each page. Check the answers together. Some of the pages have a quilt pattern on them. After your child has completed the problems, have him or her color the quilt according to the directions at the bottom of the page.

Keep On Going!
Encourage your child to add all kinds of things in your home. For example, he or she could add the number of eggs left in the carton and the number of eggs already used. Make it a fun game!

Circle a group of ten. Write the number of tens and ones.

Example

tens	ones
1	4

4.

tens	ones

1.

tens	ones

5.

tens	ones

2.

tens	ones

6.

tens	ones

3.

tens	ones

7.

tens	ones

Add. Color the picture using the color code.

Color Code

1	pink
2	white
3	black
4	brown
5	purple
6	green
7	blue
8	orange
9	yellow
10	red

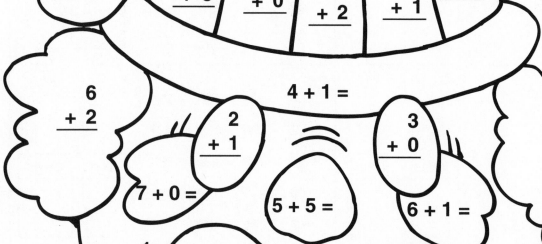

Scholastic

Add. Color the picture. Use the color key below.

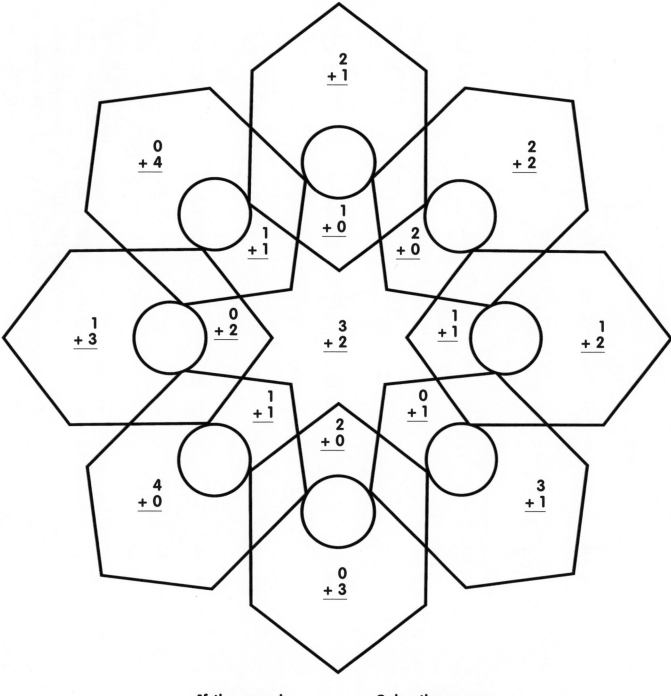

If the sum is	Color the space
1 or 2	blue
3 or 4	purple
5	red

Fill in the other spaces with colors of your choice.

Add.

1. 3
    + 0

2. 2
    + 3

3. 0
    + 2

4. 6
    + 0

5. 1
    + 2

6. 4
    + 0

7. 1
    + 5

8. 3
    + 0

9. 4
    + 2

10. 5
    + 0

11. 3
    + 1

12. 0
    + 6

13. 2
    + 1

14. 3
    + 3

15. 4
    + 1

16. 1
    + 1

17. 2
    + 2

18. 5
    + 1

19. 0
    + 0

20. 3
    + 2

Scholastic

Add.

1. 5
    +2

2. 2
    +1

3. 4
    +1

4. 3
    +4

5. 2
    +4

6. 6
    +1

7. 3
    +3

8. 1
    +5

Add!

9. 5
    +1

10. 5
     +0

11. 3
     +1

12. 7
     +0

13. 1
     +6

14. 0
     +7

15. 4
     +3

16. 2
     +2

17. 1
     +2

18. 0
     +5

19. 0
     +0

20. 4
     +2

Add.

1. 1
   +4

2. 2
   +3

3. 3
   +7

4. 3
   +3

5. 2
   +8

6. 10
   +0

7. 3
   +5

8. 6
   +2

9. 4
   +5

10. 6
    +3

11. 2
    +7

12. 8
    +1

13. 2
    +4

14. 2
    +2

15. 1
    +8

16. 7
    +3

17. 5
    +3

18. 5
    +0

19. 6
    +4

20. 0
    +1

Scholastic

Add.

1. 6
+ 3

2. 2
+ 6

3. 5
+ 5

4. 8
+ 0

Add!

5. 8
+ 2

6. 4
+ 3

7. 2
+ 7

8. 0
+ 3

9. 2
+ 5

10. 0
+ 9

11. 5
+ 1

12. 7
+ 2

13. 4
+ 4

14. 1
+ 2

15. 9
+ 1

16. 3
+ 6

17. 6
+ 1

18. 5
+ 2

19. 0
+ 1

20. 6
+ 3

Scholastic

Add.

1. **1 + 10 =**

2. **3 + 3 =**

3. **2 + 8 =**

4. **10 + 0 =**

5. **3 + 5 =**

6. **6 + 2 =**

7. **5 + 4 =**

8. **2 + 4 =**

9. **6 + 5 =**

10. **0 + 1 =**

11. **6 + 4 =**

12. **5 + 0 =**

13. **5 + 3 =**

14. **7 + 3 =**

15. **1 + 8 =**

16. **2 + 2 =**

17. **7 + 2 =**

18. **6 + 5 =**

19. **7 + 4 =**

20. **3 + 8 =**

Add!

Scholastic

Add.

1. 9
    + 2

2. 5
    + 4

3. 10
    + 1

4. 9
    + 1

5. 3
    + 2

6. 3
    + 3

7. 9
    + 0

8. 7
    + 3

9. 3
    + 4

10. 5
     + 3

11. 4
     + 3

12. 8
     + 2

13. 5
     + 5

14. 7
     + 3

15. 6
     + 3

16. 9
     + 2

17. 5
     + 6

18. 8
     + 1

19. 6
     + 3

20. 9
     + 2

Add.

1. 6
   + 1

2. 9
   + 3

3. 9
   + 1

4. 6
   + 2

Add!

5. 4
   + 5

6. 6
   + 4

7. 10
   + 2

8. 8
   + 4

9. 3
   + 5

10. 4
    + 8

11. 12
    + 0

12. 8
    + 1

13. 5
    + 6

14. 5
    + 3

15. 9
    + 2

16. 7
    + 5

17. 8
    + 3

18. 9
    + 3

19. 7
    + 4

20. 4
    + 6

Scholastic

Add.

1. $8 + 3 =$ 2. $9 + 3 =$ 3. $5 + 4 =$

Add!

4. $10 + 2 =$ 5. $9 + 1 =$ 6. $8 + 4 =$

7. $3 + 3 =$ 8. $9 + 0 =$ 9. $7 + 3 =$

10. $3 + 4 =$ 11. $5 + 3 =$ 12. $6 + 4 =$ 13. $3 + 7 =$

14. $4 + 4 =$ 15. $8 + 2 =$ 16. $5 + 5 =$ 17. $7 + 3 =$

18. $6 + 3 =$ 19. $9 + 2 =$ 20. $6 + 6 =$

Scholastic

Add.

1. 8
   + 3

2. 5
   + 5

3. 7
   + 6

4. 6
   + 5

Add!

5. 9
   + 3

6. 6
   + 6

7. 10
   + 2

8. 5
   + 4

9. 7
   + 6

10. 5
    + 4

11. 4
    + 4

12. 5
    + 3

13. 7
    + 4

14. 6
    + 0

15. 9
    + 4

16. 8
    + 4

17. 7
    + 2

18. 3
    + 4

19. 6
    + 3

20. 10
    + 3

Scholastic

Add.

1. 7
 + 6

2. 5
 + 9

3. 5
 + 7

4. 6
 + 6

Add!

5. 4
 + 6

6. 6
 + 8

7. 9
 + 4

8. 8
 + 2

9. 7
 + 7

10. 5
 + 8

11. 4
 + 8

12. 8
 + 5

13. 6
 + 5

14. 4
 + 9

15. 3
 + 9

16. 7
 + 3

17. 5
 + 6

18. 8
 + 6

19. 9
 + 3

20. 7
 + 5

Scholastic

Add.

1. $3 + 4 =$ 2. $4 + 9 =$ 3. $6 + 3 =$

Add!

4. $4 + 5 =$ 5. $5 + 9 =$ 6. $7 + 6 =$

7. $5 + 2 =$ 8. $9 + 3 =$ 9. $6 + 8 =$

10. $5 + 5 =$ 11. $6 + 7 =$ 12. $10 + 4 =$ 13. $8 + 3 =$

14. $9 + 1 =$ 15. $6 + 5 =$ 16. $8 + 6 =$ 17. $6 + 4 =$

18. $9 + 2 =$ 19. $9 + 4 =$ 20. $6 + 6 =$

Add.

1. 8
   +3

2. 8
   +5

3. 9
   +5

4. 3
   +9

5. 8
   +6

6. 5
   +9

7. 9
   +4

8. 6
   +5

9. 4
   +8

10. 7
    +4

11. 7
    +3

12. 7
    +7

13. 9
    +3

14. 6
    +8

15. 2
    +8

16. 7
    +5

17. 3
    +8

18. 5
    +8

19. 7
    +6

20. 4
    +6

Add.

1. $8 + 3 =$ 2. $5 + 5 =$ 3. $9 + 4 =$

4. $9 + 3 =$ 5. $6 + 8 =$ 6. $7 + 6 =$

Add!

7. $7 + 3 =$ 8. $6 + 6 =$ 9. $8 + 4 =$

10. $9 + 1 =$ 11. $7 + 5 =$ 12. $9 + 2 =$ 13. $7 + 8 =$

14. $8 + 2 =$ 15. $4 + 5 =$ 16. $8 + 6 =$ 17. $6 + 3 =$

18. $7 + 7 =$ 19. $9 + 5 =$ 20. $5 + 6 =$

Scholastic

Add.

1. $\begin{array}{r} 9 \\ + 3 \\ \hline \end{array}$
2. $\begin{array}{r} 8 \\ + 7 \\ \hline \end{array}$
3. $\begin{array}{r} 9 \\ + 2 \\ \hline \end{array}$
4. $\begin{array}{r} 6 \\ + 6 \\ \hline \end{array}$

5. $\begin{array}{r} 8 \\ + 2 \\ \hline \end{array}$
6. $\begin{array}{r} 7 \\ + 4 \\ \hline \end{array}$
7. $\begin{array}{r} 6 \\ + 5 \\ \hline \end{array}$
8. $\begin{array}{r} 8 \\ + 6 \\ \hline \end{array}$

Add!

9. $\begin{array}{r} 8 \\ + 5 \\ \hline \end{array}$
10. $\begin{array}{r} 9 \\ + 8 \\ \hline \end{array}$
11. $\begin{array}{r} 8 \\ + 8 \\ \hline \end{array}$
12. $\begin{array}{r} 7 \\ + 5 \\ \hline \end{array}$

13. $\begin{array}{r} 8 \\ + 6 \\ \hline \end{array}$
14. $\begin{array}{r} 8 \\ + 9 \\ \hline \end{array}$
15. $\begin{array}{r} 7 \\ + 7 \\ \hline \end{array}$
16. $\begin{array}{r} 7 \\ + 6 \\ \hline \end{array}$

17. $\begin{array}{r} 6 \\ + 4 \\ \hline \end{array}$
18. $\begin{array}{r} 5 \\ + 5 \\ \hline \end{array}$
19. $\begin{array}{r} 9 \\ + 1 \\ \hline \end{array}$
20. $\begin{array}{r} 7 \\ + 8 \\ \hline \end{array}$

Add.

1. $9 + 6 =$ 2. $8 + 3 =$ 3. $9 + 3 =$

4. $8 + 6 =$ 5. $5 + 5 =$ 6. $6 + 5 =$

Add!

7. $7 + 6 =$ 8. $8 + 2 =$ 9. $7 + 5 =$

10. $9 + 9 =$ 11. $6 + 4 =$ 12. $7 + 7 =$ 13. $9 + 8 =$

14. $9 + 4 =$ 15. $6 + 6 =$ 16. $8 + 5 =$ 17. $9 + 7 =$

18. $6 + 3 =$ 19. $9 + 5 =$ 20. $8 + 8 =$

Scholastic

Add.

1. 3
   +9

2. 12
   +6

3. 9
   +7

4. 6
   +5

Add!

5. 7
   +8

6. 10
   +8

7. 8
   +6

8. 2
   +8

9. 7
   +7

10. 5
    +8

11. 11
    +7

12. 7
    +9

13. 9
    +6

14. 5
    +9

15. 6
    +7

16. 7
    +4

17. 9
    +8

18. 6
    +4

19. 8
    +3

20. 8
    +8

Add. To show the frog's path across the pond, color each lily pad green if the sum is greater than ten.

10 + 1 =

6 + 4 =

6 + 9 =

5 + 2 =

7 + 0 =

9 + 2 =

5 + 5 =

10 + 4 =

3 + 7 =

7 + 6 =

4 + 3 =

5 + 4 =

3 + 8 =

2 + 2 =

8 + 8 =

 How many leaps did the frog take across the pond? _____

Scholastic

Add down and across to find the missing number.

A.

2	4	6
3	1	4
5	5	10

B.

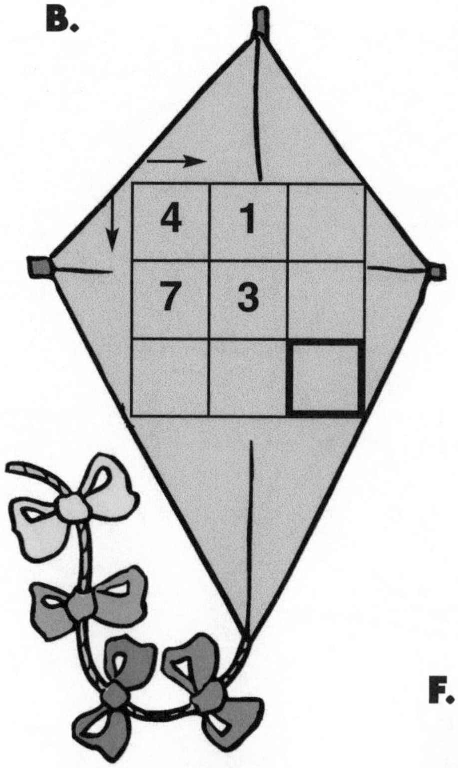

4	1	
7	3	

C.

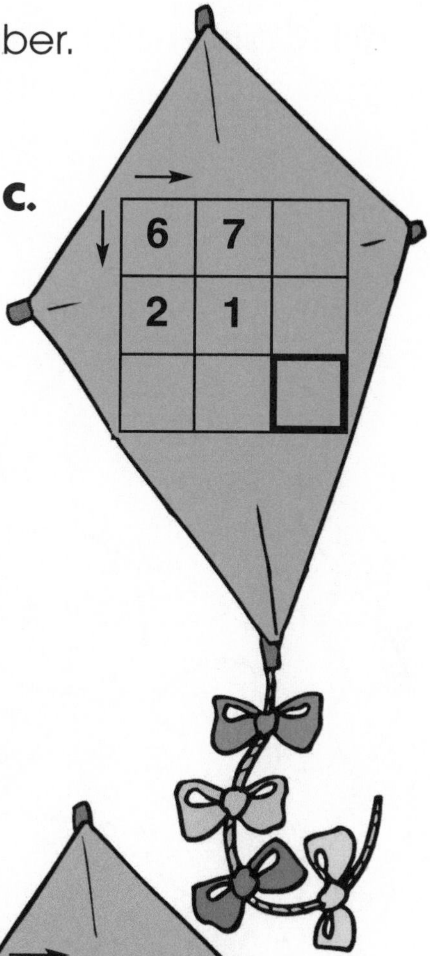

6	7	
2	1	

D.

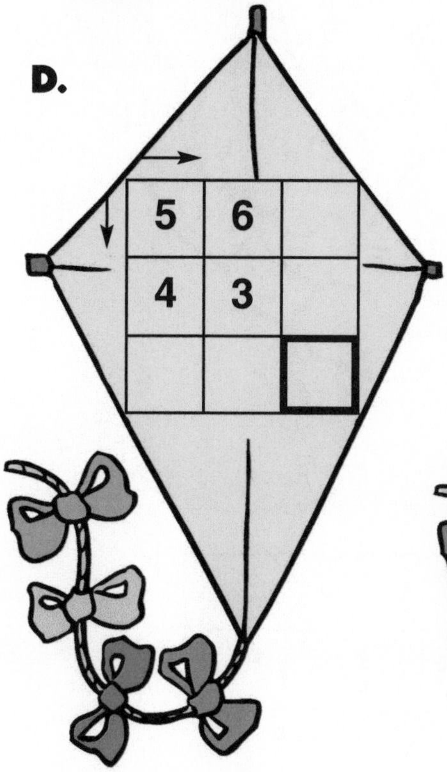

5	6	
4	3	

E.

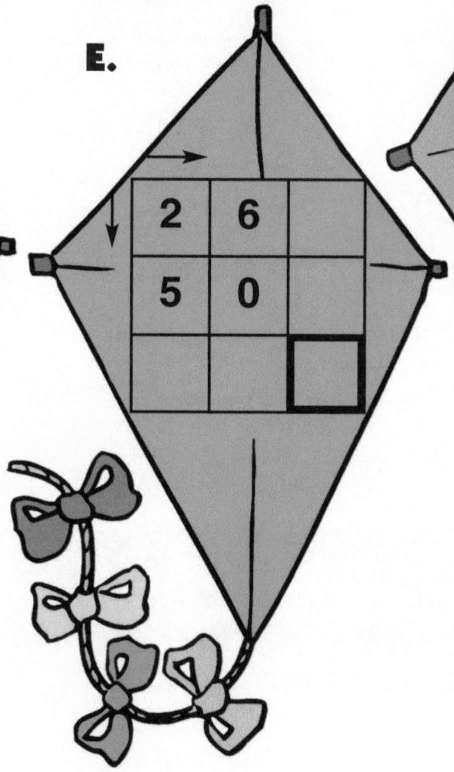

2	6	
5	0	

F.

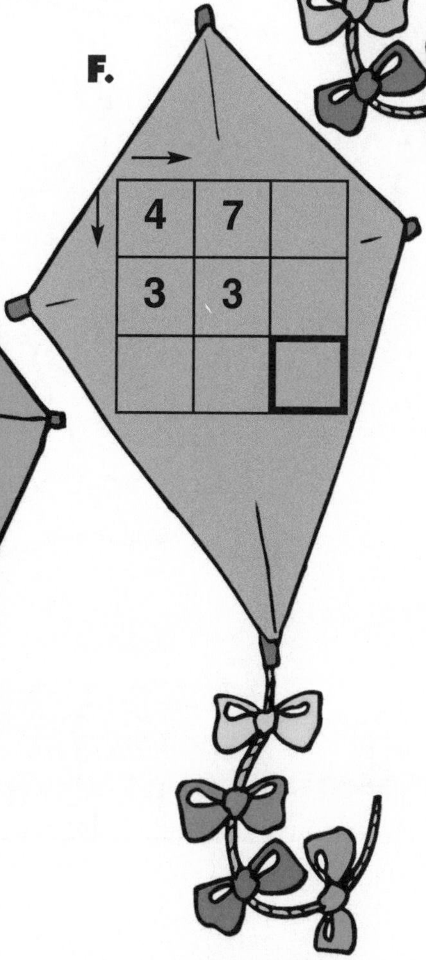

4	7	
3	3	

Add. Color the picture using the color code.

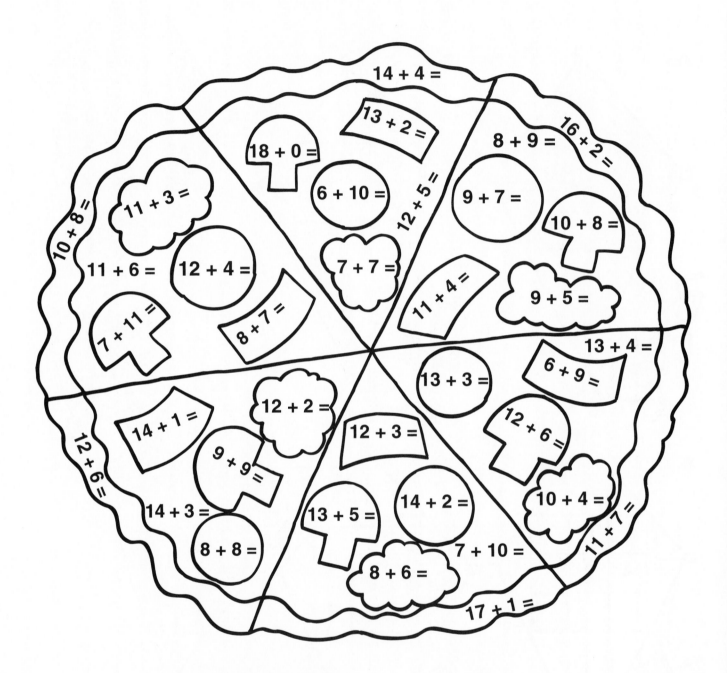

Color Code	brown	green	red	yellow	tan
	14	15	16	17	18

Add. Color the picture. Use the color key below.

40 + 36 =	12 + 13	32 + 45 =

52 + 30	13 + 10	42 + 6	20 + 45	10 + 10	31 + 52

| 30
+ 45 | 13
+ 20 |

| 12
+ 10 | 14
+ 11 | 12
+ 13 |

| 19
+ 10 | 19
+ 42 |

| 81
+ 16 | 23
+ 36 | 25
+ 16 | 50
+ 29 |

| 13
+ 11 | 11
+ 10 |

| 90 + 10 = | 10
+ 10 | 45 + 45 = |

If the sum is between	Color the space
1 and 25	blue
26 and 50	orange
51 and 75	purple
76 and 100	red

Fill in the other spaces with colors of your choice.

Scholastic

Reading & Math • Grade 1 (231)

Add. Color the picture. Use the color key below.

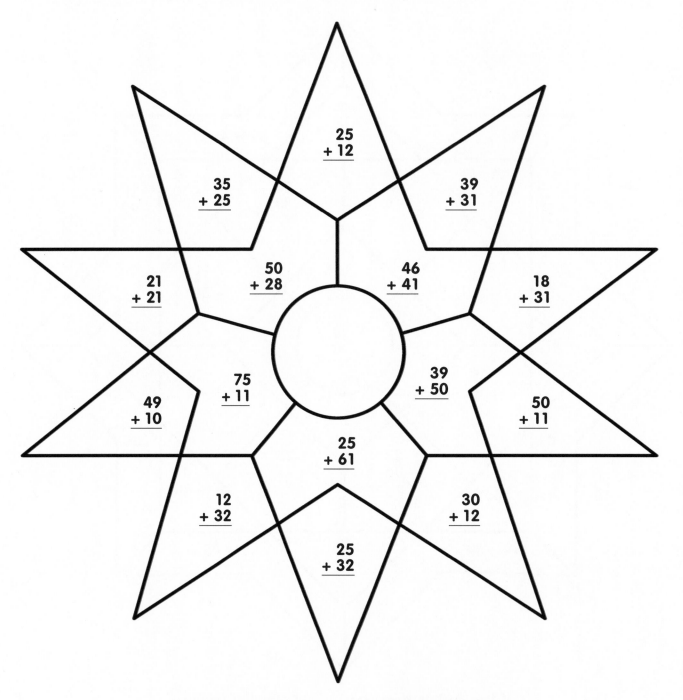

If the sum is between	Color the space
1 and 50	orange
51 and 70	yellow
71 and 100	red

Fill in the other spaces with colors of your choice.

Add. Color the picture. Use the color key below.

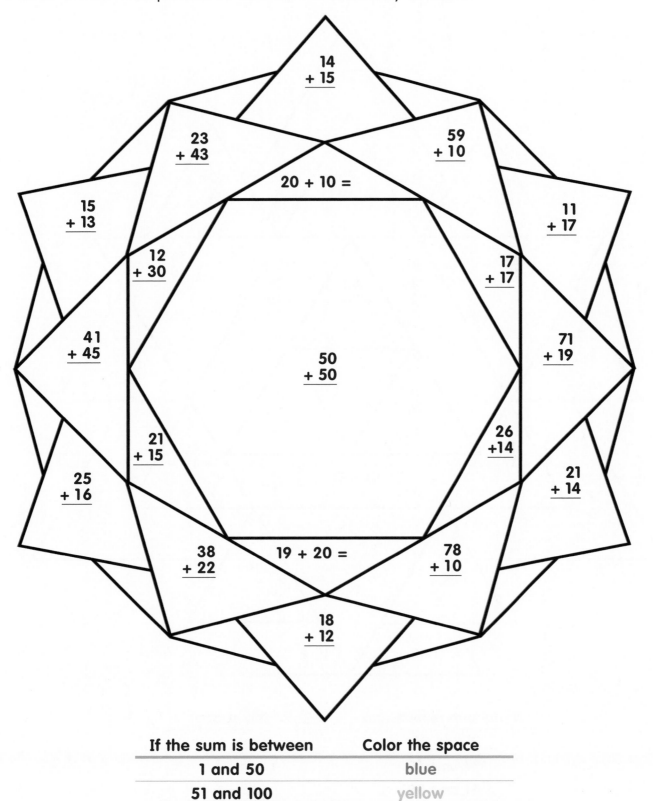

If the sum is between	Color the space
1 and 50	blue
51 and 100	yellow

Fill in the other spaces with colors of your choice.

Add. Color the picture. Use the color key below.

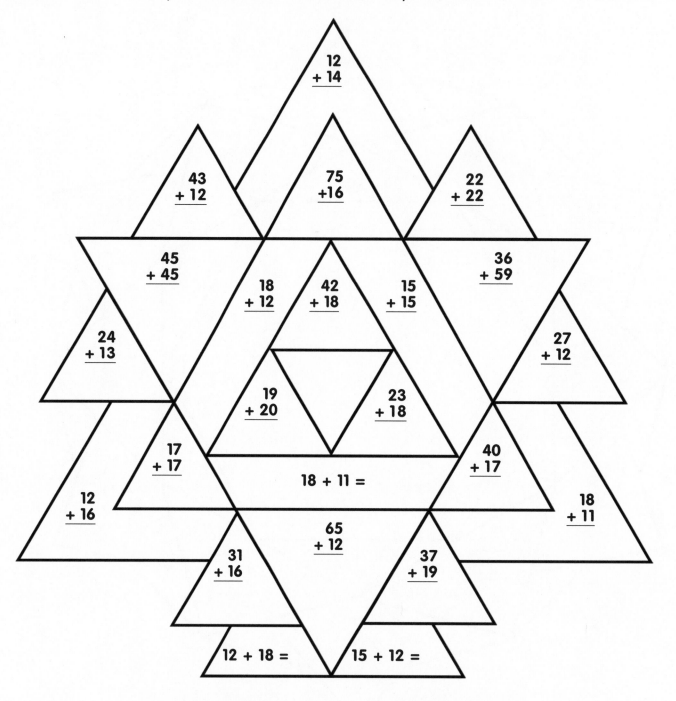

If the sum is between	Color the space
1 and 30	purple
31 and 60	orange
61 and 99	yellow

Fill in the other spaces with colors of your choice.

Scholastic

Add. Color the picture. Use the color key below.

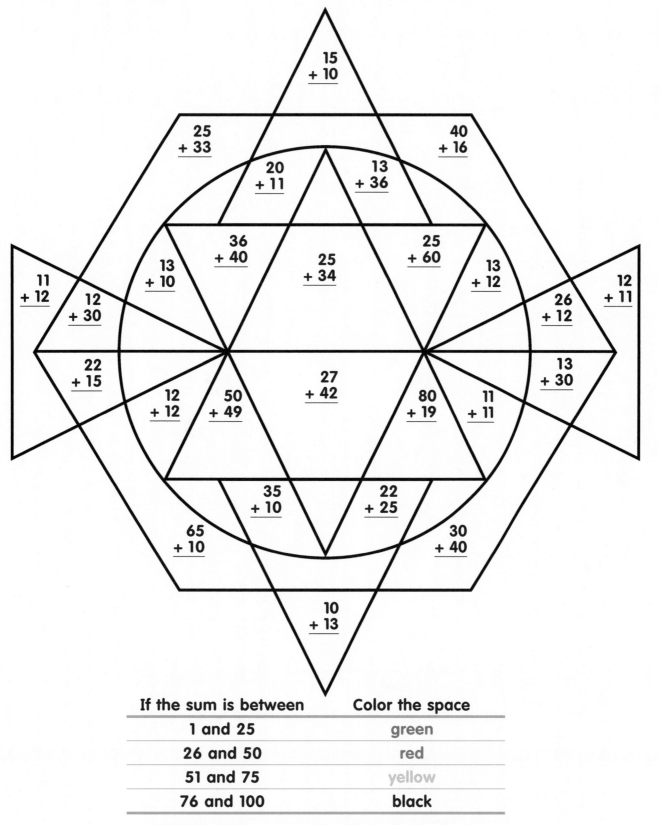

If the sum is between	Color the space
1 and 25	green
26 and 50	red
51 and 75	yellow
76 and 100	black

Fill in the other spaces with colors of your choice.

Scholastic

Addition Practice Test

Fill in the bubble next to the correct answer.

1. 10 + 12 =

    ○ **A**   32

    ○ **B**   22

    ○ **C**   15

    ○ **D**   37

2.
$$27 \atop + 22$$

    ○ **F**   49

    ○ **G**   45

    ○ **H**   22

    ○ **J**   26

3.
$$36 \atop + 12$$

    ○ **A**   46

    ○ **B**   37

    ○ **C**   48

    ○ **D**   53

4.
$$33 \atop + 14$$

    ○ **F**   46

    ○ **G**   47

    ○ **H**   48

    ○ **J**   53

Scholastic

Addition Practice Test

Fill in the bubble next to the correct answer.

5.
```
   62
 + 27
```

- ○ **A** 80
- ○ **B** 89
- ○ **C** 70
- ○ **D** 18

7.
```
   54
 + 22
```

- ○ **A** 76
- ○ **B** 78
- ○ **C** 79
- ○ **D** 68

6.
```
   11
 + 37
```

- ○ **F** 40
- ○ **G** 49
- ○ **H** 48
- ○ **J** 59

8.
```
   12
 + 15
```

- ○ **F** 27
- ○ **G** 37
- ○ **H** 29
- ○ **J** 31

Addition Practice Test

Fill in the bubble next to the correct answer.

9.
$$\begin{array}{r} 16 \\ + 33 \\ \hline \end{array}$$

○ **A** 64

○ **B** 45

○ **C** 49

○ **D** 53

11.
$$\begin{array}{r} 51 \\ + 25 \\ \hline \end{array}$$

○ **A** 67

○ **B** 77

○ **C** 76

○ **D** 46

10.
$$\begin{array}{r} 46 \\ + 42 \\ \hline \end{array}$$

○ **F** 85

○ **G** 88

○ **H** 105

○ **J** 75

12.
$$\begin{array}{r} 63 \\ + 25 \\ \hline \end{array}$$

○ **F** 48

○ **G** 68

○ **H** 78

○ **J** 88

Scholastic

Subtraction

Your child will learn basic subtraction facts in this section of the workbook. He or she will learn how to subtract single- and double-digit numbers without regrouping.

What to Do

Have your child complete the problems on each page. Point out that they can check their answers by adding the answer to the second number. If that answer matches the first number, they know the answer is correct. For example 6 − 2 = 4/4 + 2 = 6.

Some of the pages have a quilt pattern on them. After your child has completed the problems, have him or her color the quilt according to the directions on the bottom of the page. This might be a page you want to frame and hang in your child's room.

Keep On Going

Play a subtraction game with your child. Each make up problems for the other to solve. You both should check your answers by adding the answer to the second number. Point out to your child how useful subtraction will be when he or she is out shopping!

Subtract.

1. **6 – 2 =**

2. **3 – 1 =**

3. **2 – 0 =**

4. **5 – 1 =**

5. **6 – 2 =**

6. **5 – 5 =**

7. **3 – 2 =**

8. **6 – 3 =**

9. **5 – 2 =**

10. **3 – 0 =**

11. **1 – 1 =**

12. **5 – 0 =**

13. **4 – 4 =**

14. **5 – 4 =**

15. **6 – 3 =**

16. **4 – 3 =**

17. **6 – 0 =**

18. **4 – 1 =**

19. **2 – 0 =**

20. **5 – 2 =**

Scholastic

Subtract.

1. $\begin{array}{r} 7 \\ -4 \\ \hline \end{array}$ 2. $\begin{array}{r} 6 \\ -5 \\ \hline \end{array}$ 3. $\begin{array}{r} 6 \\ -4 \\ \hline \end{array}$ 4. $\begin{array}{r} 4 \\ -2 \\ \hline \end{array}$

5. $\begin{array}{r} 7 \\ -5 \\ \hline \end{array}$ 6. $\begin{array}{r} 5 \\ -0 \\ \hline \end{array}$ 7. $\begin{array}{r} 3 \\ -3 \\ \hline \end{array}$ 8. $\begin{array}{r} 0 \\ -0 \\ \hline \end{array}$

9. $\begin{array}{r} 5 \\ -2 \\ \hline \end{array}$ 10. $\begin{array}{r} 6 \\ -2 \\ \hline \end{array}$ 11. $\begin{array}{r} 5 \\ -1 \\ \hline \end{array}$ 12. $\begin{array}{r} 7 \\ -2 \\ \hline \end{array}$

13. $\begin{array}{r} 4 \\ -4 \\ \hline \end{array}$ 14. $\begin{array}{r} 2 \\ -1 \\ \hline \end{array}$ 15. $\begin{array}{r} 7 \\ -1 \\ \hline \end{array}$ 16. $\begin{array}{r} 6 \\ -3 \\ \hline \end{array}$

17. $\begin{array}{r} 6 \\ -1 \\ \hline \end{array}$ 18. $\begin{array}{r} 5 \\ -2 \\ \hline \end{array}$ 19. $\begin{array}{r} 1 \\ -0 \\ \hline \end{array}$ 20. $\begin{array}{r} 2 \\ -1 \\ \hline \end{array}$

Scholastic

Subtract.

1. 4 − 3 =   2. 3 − 0 =   3. 7 − 2 =

Subtract!

4. 4 − 4 =   5. 5 − 0 =   6. 7 − 1 =

7. 5 − 1 =   8. 4 − 2 =   9. 7 − 0 =

10. 6 − 3 =   11. 5 − 2 =   12. 4 − 0 =   13. 2 − 0 =

14. 7 − 3 =   15. 6 − 5 =   16. 0 − 0 =   17. 6 − 2 =

18. 2 − 2 =   19. 3 − 2 =   20. 6 − 4 =

Scholastic

Subtract.

1. $\begin{array}{r} 6 \\ -\ 0 \\ \hline \end{array}$
2. $\begin{array}{r} 8 \\ -\ 2 \\ \hline \end{array}$
3. $\begin{array}{r} 7 \\ -\ 6 \\ \hline \end{array}$
4. $\begin{array}{r} 7 \\ -\ 3 \\ \hline \end{array}$

Subtract!

5. $\begin{array}{r} 8 \\ -\ 7 \\ \hline \end{array}$
6. $\begin{array}{r} 5 \\ -\ 3 \\ \hline \end{array}$
7. $\begin{array}{r} 8 \\ -\ 5 \\ \hline \end{array}$
8. $\begin{array}{r} 4 \\ -\ 2 \\ \hline \end{array}$

9. $\begin{array}{r} 5 \\ -\ 4 \\ \hline \end{array}$
10. $\begin{array}{r} 8 \\ -\ 1 \\ \hline \end{array}$
11. $\begin{array}{r} 6 \\ -\ 5 \\ \hline \end{array}$
12. $\begin{array}{r} 7 \\ -\ 2 \\ \hline \end{array}$

13. $\begin{array}{r} 6 \\ -\ 4 \\ \hline \end{array}$
14. $\begin{array}{r} 7 \\ -\ 1 \\ \hline \end{array}$
15. $\begin{array}{r} 8 \\ -\ 4 \\ \hline \end{array}$
16. $\begin{array}{r} 6 \\ -\ 6 \\ \hline \end{array}$

17. $\begin{array}{r} 7 \\ -\ 4 \\ \hline \end{array}$
18. $\begin{array}{r} 6 \\ -\ 2 \\ \hline \end{array}$
19. $\begin{array}{r} 8 \\ -\ 3 \\ \hline \end{array}$
20. $\begin{array}{r} 7 \\ -\ 7 \\ \hline \end{array}$

Scholastic

Subtract.

1. $6 - 5 =$ 2. $4 - 4 =$ 3. $5 - 1 =$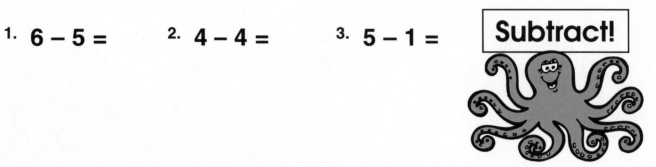
Subtract!

4. $7 - 5 =$ 5. $8 - 5 =$ 6. $7 - 7 =$

7. $5 - 2 =$ 8. $2 - 2 =$ 9. $6 - 6 =$

10. $8 - 2 =$ 11. $8 - 3 =$ 12. $8 - 4 =$ 13. $7 - 4 =$

14. $7 - 3 =$ 15. $8 - 0 =$ 16. $5 - 5 =$ 17. $8 - 1 =$

18. $8 - 6 =$ 19. $5 - 3 =$ 20. $7 - 6 =$

Subtract.

1.   9
   − 3

2.   8
   − 5

3.   9
   − 5

4.   8
   − 1

Subtract!

5.   6
   − 5

6.   7
   − 1

7.   9
   − 7

8.   8
   − 4

9.   5
   − 4

10.   7
   − 3

11.   6
   − 2

12.   7
   − 2

13.   9
   − 4

14.   9
   − 2

15.   9
   − 1

16.   9
   − 6

17.   8
   − 1

18.   7
   − 1

19.   9
   − 1

20.   8
   − 4

Scholastic

Subtract.

1. $9 - 9 =$ 2. $7 - 5 =$ 3. $8 - 8 =$

4. $9 - 4 =$ 5. $5 - 3 =$ 6. $8 - 2 =$ Subtract!

7. $7 - 4 =$ 8. $9 - 6 =$ 9. $8 - 3 =$

10. $9 - 0 =$ 11. $7 - 2 =$ 12. $9 - 3 =$ 13. $9 - 2 =$

14. $6 - 5 =$ 15. $8 - 1 =$ 16. $7 - 0 =$ 17. $4 - 4 =$

18. $6 - 6 =$ 19. $9 - 1 =$ 20. $9 - 5 =$

Scholastic

Subtract.

1. 8
  − 5

2. 6
  − 2

3. 10
  − 2

4. 7
  − 4

Subtract!

5. 10
  − 9

6. 7
  − 4

7. 8
  − 4

8. 7
  − 6

9. 10
  − 0

10. 9
  − 5

11. 8
  − 2

12. 8
  − 7

13. 9
  − 3

14. 10
  − 5

15. 8
  − 6

16. 10
  − 4

17. 7
  − 3

18. 10
  − 2

19. 8
  − 5

20. 6
  − 2

Scholastic

Subtract. Color the picture. Use the color key below.

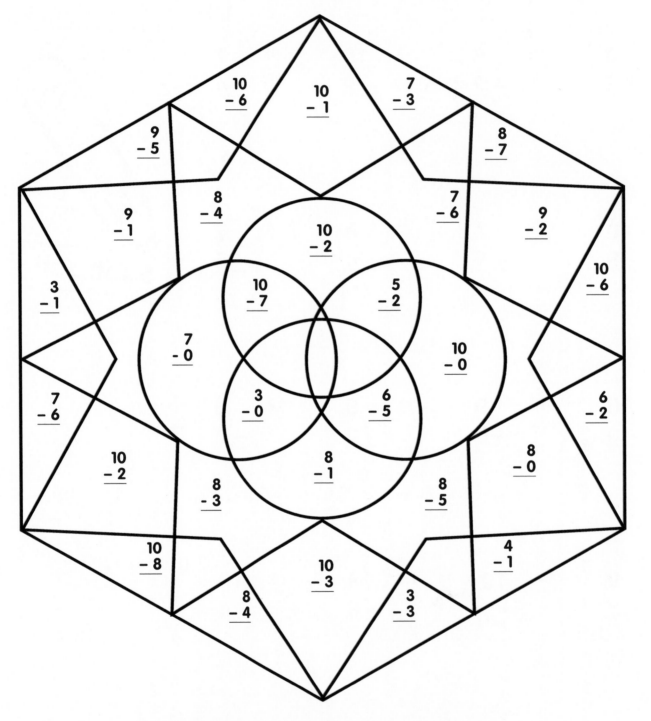

If the difference is between	Color the space
0 and 5	blue
6 and 10	red

Fill in the other spaces with colors of your choice.

Scholastic

Subtract.

1. $8 - 5 =$

2. $11 - 5 =$

3. $9 - 5 =$

Subtract!

4. $11 - 7 =$

5. $7 - 5 =$

6. $10 - 6 =$

7. $11 - 4 =$

8. $9 - 0 =$

9. $8 - 5 =$

10. $11 - 2 =$

11. $9 - 6 =$

12. $11 - 9 =$

13. $10 - 8 =$

14. $7 - 6 =$

15. $10 - 7 =$

16. $11 - 3 =$

17. $9 - 8 =$

18. $8 - 6 =$

19. $11 - 1 =$

20. $9 - 2 =$

Scholastic

Subtract.

1. 9
   − 2

2. 12
   − 6

3. 11
   − 9

4. 8
   − 3

5. 10
   − 6

6. 12
   − 4

7. 10
   − 1

8. 11
   − 5

9. 8
   − 6

10. 12
    − 8

11. 9
    − 3

12. 11
    − 6

13. 10
    − 4

14. 12
    − 5

15. 9
    − 8

16. 7
    − 6

17. 8
    − 5

18. 10
    − 7

19. 12
    − 4

20. 8
    − 2

Scholastic

Subtract. Color the picture. Use the color key below.

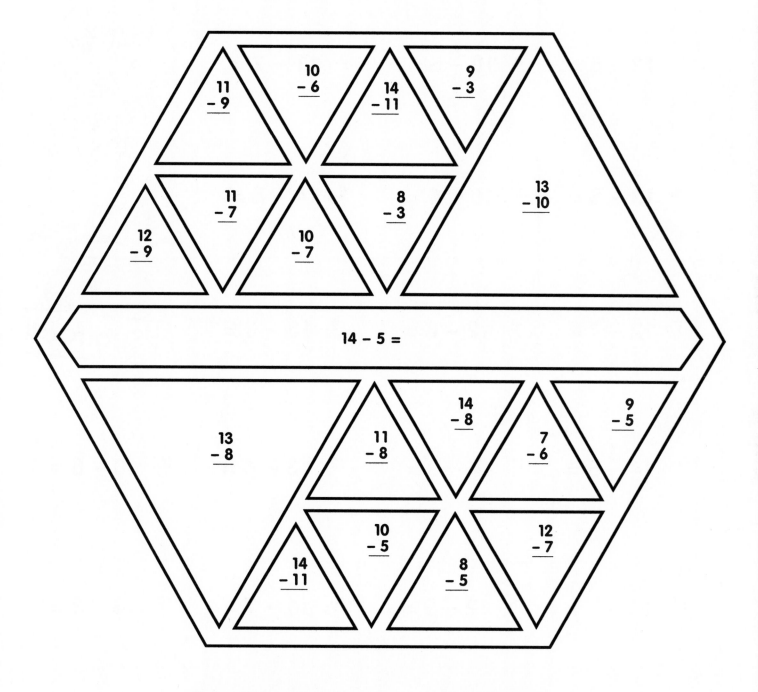

If the difference is between	Color the space
1 and 3	red
4 and 6	green
7 and 9	black

Fill in the other spaces with colors of your choice.

Subtract.

1. 12 – 6 =   2. 10 – 6 =   3. 11 – 2 =

4. 13 – 6 =   5. 10 – 4 =   6. 14 – 8 =

7. 12 – 7 =   8. 12 – 8 =   9. 13 – 5 =

Subtract!

10. 14 – 5 =   11. 14 – 9 =   12. 13 – 4 =   13. 10 – 8 =

14. 13 – 7 =   15. 12 – 9 =   16. 11 – 7 =   17. 13 – 8 =

18. 14 – 6 =   19. 12 – 5 =   20. 14 – 7 =

Scholastic

Subtract.

1. 13
   − 8

2. 12
   − 4

3. 11
   − 7

4. 14
   − 7

Subtract!

5. 13
   − 7

6. 14
   − 6

7. 11
   − 4

8. 10
   − 3

9. 12
   − 7

10. 13
    − 5

11. 11
    − 5

12. 14
    − 9

13. 13
    − 9

14. 8
    − 7

15. 10
    − 5

16. 12
    − 9

17. 13
    − 7

18. 10
    − 4

19. 12
    − 3

20. 13
    − 4

Scholastic

Subtract.

1. 15
    − 9

2. 10
    − 6

3. 14
    − 5

4. 15
    − 7

Subtract!

5. 13
    − 9

6. 12
    − 6

7. 12
    − 7

8. 10
    − 9

9. 13
    − 6

10. 13
    − 7

11. 15
    − 6

12. 14
    − 7

13. 12
    − 8

14. 15
    − 9

15. 14
    − 6

16. 15
    − 5

17. 12
    − 4

18. 13
    − 8

19. 15
    − 8

20. 13
    − 5

Scholastic

Break the Code

Subtract.

A. 6
− 2

4

B. 13
− 7

C. 17
− 7

D. 18
− 9

E. 15
− 8

F. 11
− 9

G. 9
− 4

H. 14
− 6

I. 11
− 8

J. 7
− 6

Use the answers above to solve each problem.

K.

L.

M.

N.

O.

P.

Q.

Scholastic

Subtract.

Subtract!

1.	13 − 7	2.	15 − 6	3.	12 − 8	4.	12 − 6

5.	11 − 9	6.	12 − 5	7.	17 − 9	8.	11 − 8

9.	14 − 9	10.	14 − 5	11.	18 − 9	12.	13 − 9

13.	14 − 6	14.	16 − 8	15.	11 − 3	16.	14 − 8

17.	15 − 7	18.	15 − 8	19.	12 − 9	20.	11 − 2

Subtract.

1. 12
   − 4

2. 10
   − 8

3. 13
   − 5

4. 10
   − 2

Subtract!

5. 17
   − 8

6. 11
   − 7

7. 16
   − 8

8. 14
   − 9

9. 18
   − 9

10. 13
    − 7

11. 11
    − 4

12. 11
    − 2

13. 10
    − 5

14. 12
    − 6

15. 10
    − 9

16. 14
    − 6

17. 15
    − 9

18. 11
    − 8

19. 16
    − 7

20. 12
    − 5

Scholastic

Subtract.

1. 11
  − 7

2. 13
  − 5

3. 10
  − 8

4. 12
  − 4

5. 14
  − 9

6. 16
  − 8

7. 10
  − 2

8. 17
  − 8

Subtract!

9. 11
  − 8

10. 15
   − 9

11. 14
   − 6

12. 10
   − 9

13. 12
   − 6

14. 13
   − 7

15. 15
   − 7

16. 14
   − 8

17. 12
   − 9

18. 15
   − 8

19. 16
   − 7

20. 12
   − 5

Scholastic

Subtract. Color the picture. Use the color key below.

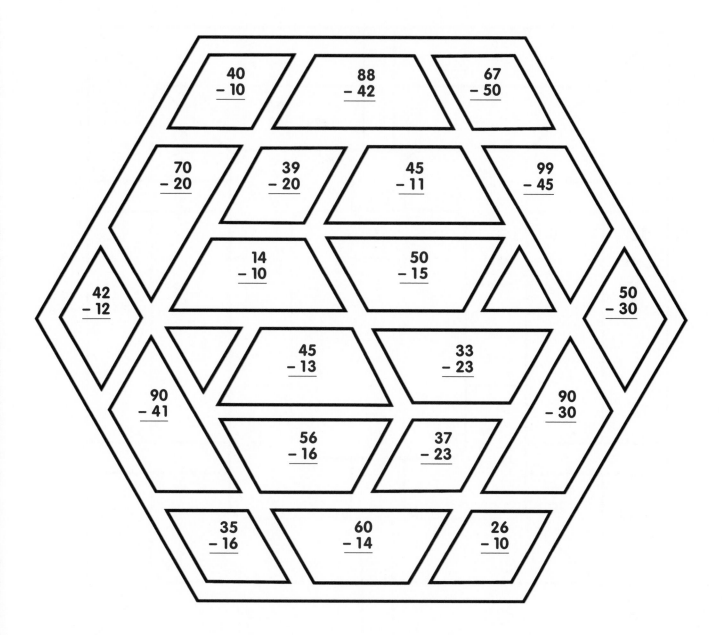

If the difference is between	Color the space
1 and 15	yellow
16 and 30	pink
31 and 45	purple
46 and 60	blue

Fill in the other spaces with colors of your choice.

Scholastic

Subtract. Color the picture. Use the color key below.

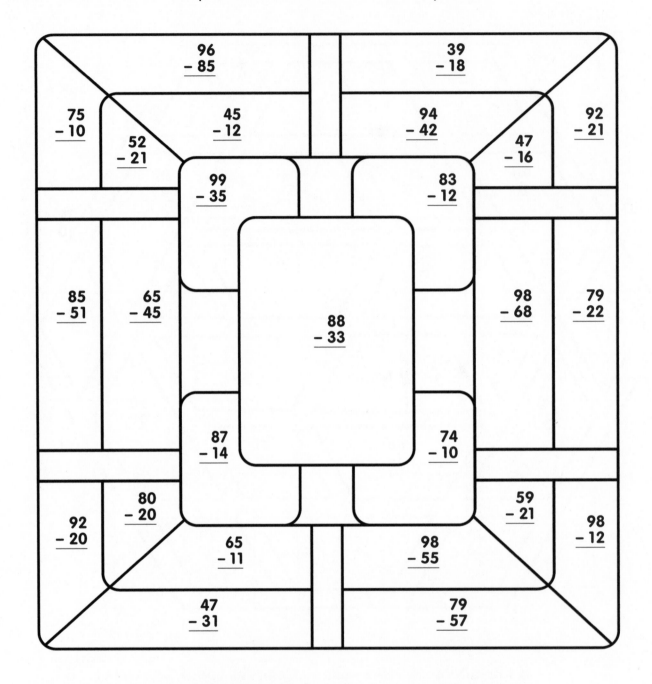

If the difference is between	Color the space
1 and 30	red
31 and 60	green
61 and 90	orange

Fill in the other spaces with colors of your choice.

Subtract. Color the picture. Use the color key below.

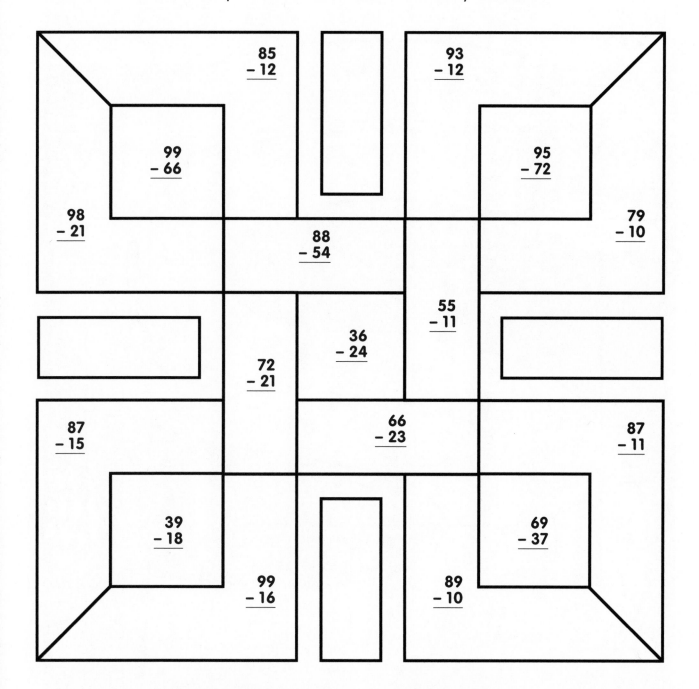

If the difference is between	Color the space
1 and 33	yellow
34 and 66	blue
67 and 99	purple

Fill in the other spaces with colors of your choice.

Add or subtract. The race car that ends with the highest number wins the race!

car 1

car 2

7 + 2 = ___ − 4 = ___ − 3 = ___ + 9 = ___

12 − 3 = ___ − 6 = ___ + 2 = ___ + 9 = ___ + 5 = ___

− 8 = ___ + 4 = ___ + 7 = ___ − 9 = ___ + 3 = ___ − 2 = ___ + 7 = ___

− 8 = ___ + 4 = ___ + 1 = ___ − 9 = ___ + 9 = ___

+ 1 = ___ − 11 = ___ − 5 = ___ + 13 = ___ − 7 = ___ + 3 = ___

− 8 = ___ + 2 = ___ + 3 = ___ − 3 = ___

 Color the winning race car blue.

Scholastic

Add or subtract. Then follow the maze through the even answers.

13 − 6 =

16 − 9 =

4 + 5 =

Start

2 + 2 =

14 − 8 =

10 − 7 =

3 + 7 =

13 − 5 =

9 + 4 =

15 − 6 =

16 − 6 =

11 + 3 =

17 − 8 =

18 − 6 =

7 + 5 =

5 + 2 =

8 + 3 =

9 + 9 =

Color a box on the graph for each item in the picture. The first one
has been done for you.

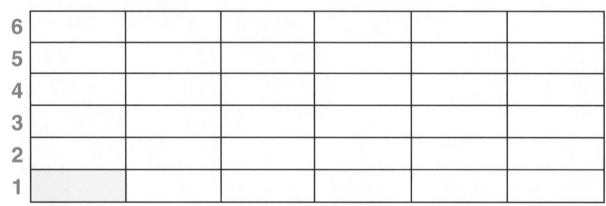

Use the graph to solve the problems.

A. How many and altogether? $6 \oplus 2 = 8$

B. How many and  in all? ____ + ____ = ____

C. How many more than ? ____ + ____ = ____

Scholastic

Color a box on the graph for each item in the picture. The first one has been done for you.

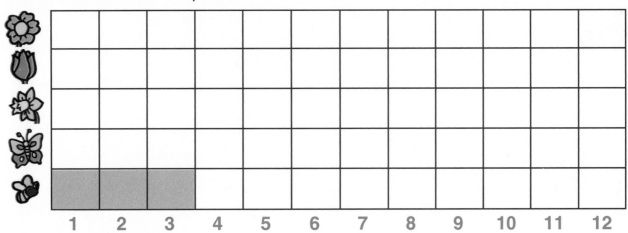

Use the graph to solve the problems.

A. Which flower is found the most?

B. How many and altogether? _____ + _____ = _____

C. How many more than ? _____ - _____ = _____

D. How many insects in all? _____ + _____ = _____

E. How many more than ? _____ - _____ = _____

F. How many and altogether? _____ + _____ = _____

Subtraction Practice Test

Fill in the bubble next to the correct answer.

1. $15 - 2 =$

    ○ A   13

    ○ B   9

    ○ C   10

    ○ D   11

2.   27
   − 16

    ○ F   7

    ○ G   8

    ○ H   11

    ○ J   10

3.   54
   − 23

    ○ A   35

    ○ B   25

    ○ C   38

    ○ D   31

4. $9 - 5 =$

    ○ F   4

    ○ G   6

    ○ H   3

    ○ J   5

Subtraction Practice Test

Fill in the bubble next to the correct answer.

5. 27 – 13 =

○ **A** 13

○ **B** 14

○ **C** 15

○ **D** 16

7. 78
      – 56

○ **A** 22

○ **B** 24

○ **C** 32

○ **D** 16

6. 47
      – 26

○ **F** 15

○ **G** 16

○ **H** 17

○ **J** 21

8. 16
      – 9

○ **F** 8

○ **G** 7

○ **H** 6

○ **J** 10

Addition/Subtraction Practice Test

Fill in the bubble next to the correct answer.

9.   60
      + 27

- ○ A   85
- ○ B   87
- ○ C   75
- ○ D   65

11.   55
       - 34

- ○ A   22
- ○ B   21
- ○ C   19
- ○ D   20

10.   43
       + 24

- ○ F   63
- ○ G   67
- ○ H   81
- ○ J   93

12.   57
       - 24

- ○ F   25
- ○ G   38
- ○ H   33
- ○ J   42

Scholastic

Addition/Subtraction Practice Test

Choose a sticker to place here.

Fill in the bubble next to the correct answer.

13.
$$\begin{array}{r} 82 \\ + \ 3 \\ \hline \end{array}$$

- ○ **A**   85
- ○ **B**   105
- ○ **C**   75
- ○ **D**   64

14.
$$\begin{array}{r} 74 \\ - \ 62 \\ \hline \end{array}$$

- ○ **F**   9
- ○ **G**   13
- ○ **H**   6
- ○ **J**   12

15.
$$\begin{array}{r} 97 \\ - \ 56 \\ \hline \end{array}$$

- ○ **A**   34
- ○ **B**   43
- ○ **C**   41
- ○ **D**   39

16.
$$\begin{array}{r} 57 \\ - \ 3 \\ \hline \end{array}$$

- ○ **F**   54
- ○ **G**   49
- ○ **H**   36
- ○ **J**   26

Scholastic

Time & Money

"What time is it?" "How much change should I get back?" These are common, everyday questions that everyone asks. In this section, your child will be introduced to concepts related to telling time and understanding money. Both are important life skills.

What to Do

Read the problems with your child. Then have him or her solve the problems. Check the answers together. Praise your child for a job well done!

Keep On Going!

- Encourage your child to make a daily schedule, listing the time each activity will take place. For example: the time he or she will get up, eat breakfast, catch the school bus, have lunch, and so on. This schedule could become very important when special appointments/events (doctor, ballet lessons, hockey games, etc.) are scheduled.

- Play "store" with your child. Place money values on things around the house. Make a 5- or 10-dollar bill. Have your child go shopping. Then have him or her figure out how much money was spent and how much change he or she should get back.

Read the problem then answer the question.

7. I have one coin in my pocket.

My coin is a silver coin.

My coin is larger than a dime.

My coin is less than 10¢.

What is the change in my pocket?

_____

Read the problem then answer the question.

8. I have two coins in my pocket.

Both coins are silver.

The value of my coins is 20¢.

What is the change in my pocket?

_____

Read the problem then answer the question.

9. I have three different coins in my pocket.

I have two silver coins and one brown coin.

The value of each of my coins is less than 25¢.

What is the change in my pocket?

_____

Read the problem then answer the question.

10. I have less than 25¢ in my pocket.

I have four coins.

My coins are silver.

What is the change in my pocket?

_____

Time & Money Practice Test

Fill in the bubble next to the correct answer.

1. You have two silver coins. They are equal in value. They add up to more than 11 cents. How much money do you have?

   ○ **A**   10 cents

   ○ **B**   12 cents

   ○ **C**   20 cents

   ○ **D**   15 cents

2. You have two silver coins and five copper coins. You have more than 25 cents. How much money do you have?

   ○ **F**   15 cents

   ○ **G**   55 cents

   ○ **H**   25 cents

   ○ **J**   45 cents

3. You have three silver coins. Each one has a different value. How much money do you have?

   ○ **A**   40 cents

   ○ **B**   60 cents

   ○ **C**   25 cents

   ○ **D**   43 cents

Time & Money Practice Test

Fill in the bubble next to the correct answer

4. What time does the clock show?

○ **A**   10:00

○ **B**   7:00

○ **C**   6:00

○ **D**   5:30

5. What time does the clock show?

○ **F**   10:00

○ **G**   11:00

○ **H**   1:00

○ **J**   7:00

6. What time comes after two o'clock, but before four o'clock?

○ **A**   12:00

○ **B**   3:00

○ **C**   5:00

○ **D**   6:00

Scholastic

Get Ready for
Grade 2

In this section of the workbook, your child will get a preview of some of the new skills he or she will learn in Grade 2. The activity pages in this section were chosen to help your child develop the skills necessary to be successful. Here are some of the skills and concepts covered:

- writing the upper- and lowercase cursive alphabet
- identifying and using compound words
- identifying words that begin with each letter of the alphabet
- understanding and using special words
- understanding and using homophones
- identifying words with long and short vowels
- understanding the concept of antonyms and synonyms
- understanding the concept of analogies
- understanding and using key grammar skills: common nouns and irregular verbs
- understanding and using key mechanics of writing skills: quotation marks
- understanding some key reading skills such as using context clues and compare and contrast
- understanding concepts related to addition
- understanding concepts related to subtraction
- understanding concepts related to multiplication
- understanding concepts related to time and money
- understanding concepts related to measurement

$\mathcal{A}\,a$

Trace and write.

$\mathcal{A}\,\mathcal{A}$

$a\quad a$

$\mathcal{A}\,a$

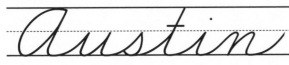

$\mathcal{A}ustin$

$ant\qquad\qquad arid$

$\mathcal{A}l\;and\;\mathcal{A}nn\;act$

$in\;\mathcal{A}ustralia.$

Scholastic

B b

Trace and write.

B B

b b

B b

Boise

bib   baby

Bob bakes brownies

in Bakersfield.

Scholastic

Cc

Trace and write.

CC

cc

Cc

Chicago

city   cute

Christy and Celia

chat in Cancun.

Scholastic

A **compound word** *is a word made by joining two words together to make a new word.*

Complete the crossword puzzle with the missing part of each compound word. Use the Word Bank to help you.

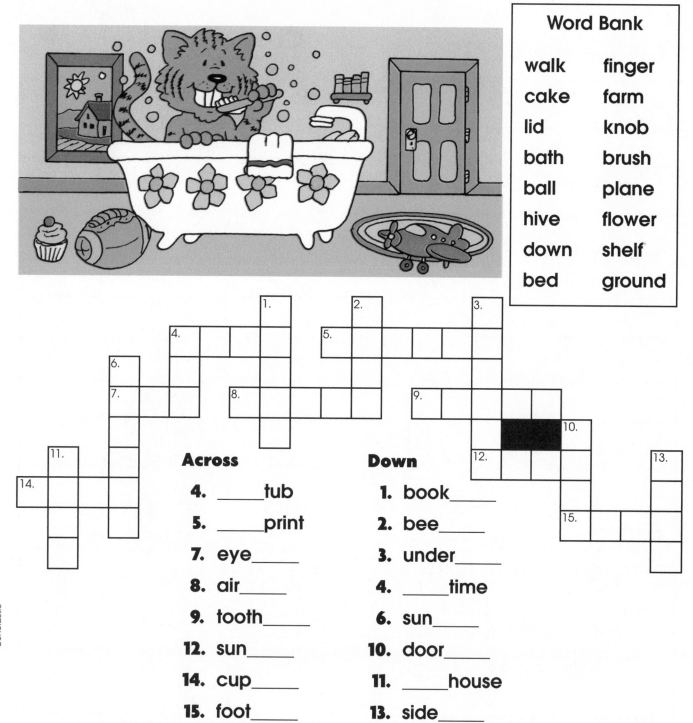

Word Bank	
walk	finger
cake	farm
lid	knob
bath	brush
ball	plane
hive	flower
down	shelf
bed	ground

Across

4. _____tub

5. _____print

7. eye_____

8. air_____

9. tooth_____

12. sun_____

14. cup_____

15. foot_____

Down

1. book_____

2. bee_____

3. under_____

4. _____time

6. sun_____

10. door_____

11. _____house

13. side_____

Read each sentence. Circle the word that means the opposite of the underlined word.

1. We found some <u>large</u> starfish at the beach.

      blue   small   dirty

2. Please do not run <u>inside.</u>

      outside   around   after

3. My friends and I are always <u>together</u>.

      near   apart   quietly

4. You can <u>stay</u> if you want to.

      talk   rest   leave

5. Do not <u>sit</u> while he is speaking.

      talk   stand   cry

6. My grades are getting <u>better</u>.

      higher   worse   as good as

7. This is a very <u>dark</u> room.

      light   funny   old

8. <u>None</u> of the students went to the play.

      some   two   all

Scholastic

Read each sentence. Circle the word that means almost the same as the underlined word.

1. Tom was outside for <u>just</u> five minutes.

after   only   over

2. Please <u>save</u> this seat for me.

bring   buy   keep

3. The three bears lived in the <u>woods</u>.

forest   house   tent

4. Pam went to bed because she was <u>sleepy</u>.

quiet   tired   awake

5. I am <u>glad</u> to see that you have done your work.

angry   asking   happy

6. First the cat <u>sniffed</u> the food, then she ate it.

smelled   pulled   pushed

7. Mary <u>tore</u> her best dress.

mended   ripped   broke

8. The teacher <u>spoke</u> in a soft voice.

cheered   screamed   talked

Homophones *are words that sound alike but have different spellings and different meanings.*

Add or subtract letters to spell the homophone of the first word. Write the homophone that fits the sentence. The first one has been done for you.

1. deer – er + ar = __dear__   The __deer__ jumped the fence to safety.

2. two – w = _____   A duet is made of _____ singers.

3. sun – u + o = _____   The father took his _____ to the game.

4. scent – s = _____   The _____ of flowers filled the room.

5. chili – i + ly = _____   Wear a coat when it is _____.

6. their – ir + re = _____   Your books are _____ on the table.

7. know – k – w = _____   The sign says _____ swimming.

8. hair – ir + re = _____   Brush your _____ before school.

9. wee – e = _____   He was a _____ little lad.

10. here – re + ar = _____   Listen closely to _____ the directions.

11. weight – eight + ait = _____   The rock's _____ was great.

12. break – eak + ake = _____   It is time for a _____.

Scholastic

Use the words in the box to label each part of the flower and to complete the sentences below.

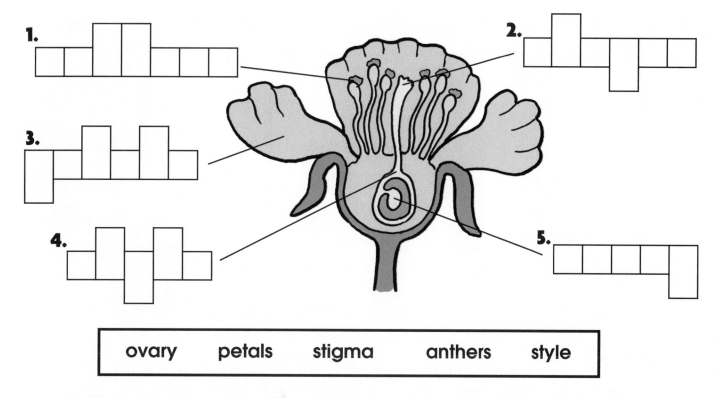

1.

2.

3.

4.

5.

| ovary | petals | stigma | anthers | style |

A flower is important in the life cycle of a plant because it contains the parts for reproduction. The colorful **6.** _ _ t _ _ _ and sepals protect the flower when it is in bud. The sticky part in the middle of the flower is the **7.** _ _ _ g _ _ . Around the stigma are **8.** _ n _ _ _ _ _ _ , which are tiny stems with knobs on top. Inside the anthers is a golden dust called pollen. In the base of the flower is the **9.** _ v _ _ _ _ . Growing out of the ovary is the **10.** _ _ y _ _ . When ripe, the anthers burst open sending out clouds of pollen. The pollen is carried to the stigma of another flower. This is called pollination.

Find the words from the word list and circle them in the puzzle below.

CAREERS WORD LIST

CHEF	FIREFIGHTER
TEACHER	BAKER
FARMER	DOCTOR
PILOT	LAWYER
CAPTAIN	DENTIST

```
F I R E F I G H T E R D
A S D R E P W C Q T F O
B A K E R I M A L E A C
X C V B N L P P K A R T
C H E F O O I T J C M O
E R T Y U T Z A H H E R
D E N T I S T I G E R D
L A W Y E R J N F R A S
```

Choose the correct word to complete each sentence.

1. A <u>leg</u> is a part of a <u>table</u>, and a <u>seat</u> is a part of a _____.
Ⓐ rug   Ⓑ chair   Ⓒ bed

2. A <u>string</u> is a part of a <u>harp</u>, and a <u>button</u> is a part of a _____.
Ⓐ shirt   Ⓑ snap   Ⓒ circle

3. A <u>screen</u> is a part of a <u>TV</u>, and a <u>hand</u> is a part of a _____.
Ⓐ broom   Ⓑ clock   Ⓒ knob

4. A <u>yolk</u> is a part of an <u>egg</u>, and a <u>pit</u> is a part of a _____.
Ⓐ peach   Ⓑ hen   Ⓒ word

5. A <u>heel</u> is a part of a <u>foot</u>, and an <u>eye</u> is a part of a _____.
Ⓐ toe   Ⓑ nose   Ⓒ face

6. A <u>stove</u> is a part of a <u>kitchen</u>, and a <u>couch</u> is a part of a _____.
Ⓐ den   Ⓑ sink   Ⓒ floor

7. A <u>wing</u> is a part of a <u>bird</u>, and a <u>sleeve</u> is a part of a _____.
Ⓐ nest   Ⓑ sweater   Ⓒ pocket

8. A <u>drawer</u> is a part of a <u>desk</u>, and a <u>pedal</u> is a part of a _____.
Ⓐ ladder   Ⓑ step   Ⓒ bike

Scholastic

When you are reading, do you get stuck on words that you don't know? Does not knowing a word make it hard to understand what you are reading? **Context clues** *can help you. Use context clues to figure out what the word is. That means think about the other words in the sentence. What clues do they give? Then ask yourself what other word would make sense there.*

What do you think the underlined word means in each sentence below? Circle the meaning that makes sense. Then rewrite each sentence using the meaning instead of the underlined word.

1. My domino has two white <u>pips</u>, and yours has five.

    baby dogs   spots   long metal tubes

_____

2. A gray <u>fulmar</u> flew by the cruise ship.

    lizard   swordfish   seabird

_____

3. The queen had a beautiful necklace made of <u>jasper</u>.

    a green stone   yellow pudding   wet snow

_____

4. My sister is the best <u>flutist</u> in the high school band.

    waitress   runner   flute player

_____

Scholastic

Kendra and her mom left their house on Oak Street to go to school. Kendra put on her safety belt. About that same time, Lacey and her mom left their house on Maple Street. On the way to school, Lacey bounced up and down on the seat watching her pigtails fly up and down in the mirror. She had forgotten to wear her safety belt. Both moms turned into the school parking lot at the same time, and they crashed into each other! Kendra was not hurt. Her safety belt kept her in her seat. But, Lacey fell forward and bumped her head HARD! She cried and cried. She had to go to the hospital and get an X ray. Lacey got well in a day or two, but she learned an important lesson!

Draw a 😊 in the correct column.

	Kendra	Lacey	both
1. driven to school by Mom			
2. wore a safety belt			
3. didn't wear a safety belt			
4. lives on Maple Street			
5. was in a wreck			
6. bumped her head			
7. got an X ray			
8. lives on Oak Street			
9. bounced up and down in the car			
10. didn't get hurt			
11. learned a lesson			

Scholastic

Common nouns *name people, places, or things.*

Help sort the cards. Some of the words are nouns. Some are not.
Circle the nouns.

Write each noun you circled under the correct heading.

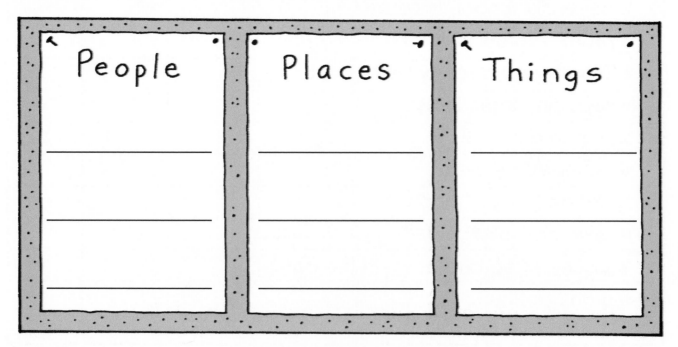

People	Places	Things

Scholastic

Irregular verbs change their spelling when they tell about the past. **Did** *is the past form of* **do** *and* **does.** **Went** *is the past form of* **go** *and* **goes.**

Read each sentence. Write present if the underlined verb tells about action now. Write past if it tells about action in the past.

Present	Past
go, goes	went
do, does	did

1 Grace <u>goes</u> to the playground. _____

2 Some other children <u>go</u>, too. _____

3 Grace <u>does</u> a scene from a story. _____

4 The children <u>do</u> the scene with her. _____

5 Grace <u>went</u> into battle as Joan of Arc. _____

6 She <u>did</u> the part of Anansi the Spider, too. _____

7 In another part, Grace <u>went</u> inside a

wooden horse. _____

8 She <u>did</u> many other parts. _____

Scholastic

Quotation marks *show the exact words someone says. They go before the speaker's first word. They also go after the speaker's last word and the end punctuation mark.*

Read each sentence. Underline the exact words the speaker says. Put the words in quotation marks. The first one is done for you.

1 Max said, "<u>Let's go on a picnic.</u>"

2 Cori replied, That's a great idea.

3 Andy asked, What should we bring?

4 Max said with a laugh, We should bring food.

5 Cori added, Yes, let's bring lots and lots of food.

6 Andy giggled and said, You're no help at all!

Finish the sentences below by writing what Max, Cori, and Andy might say next. Use quotation marks.

7 Max said, _____.

8 Cori asked, _____.

9 Andy answered, _____.

Scholastic

*If the naming part of a sentence names one, add **-s** to the action word. If the naming part names more than one, do not add **-s** to the action word.*

Read each sentence. Underline the word in parentheses ( ) that correctly completes it. Write the word on the line.

1 **Kim** _____ **a story about a monkey.** (write, writes)

2 **The monkey** _____ **his friend in the city.**
(meet, meets)

3 **The two friends** _____ **on the bus.** (ride, rides)

4 **The monkeys** _____ **for toys and presents.**
(shop, shops)

5 **The store** _____ **at 7 o'clock.** (close, closes)

6 **The monkeys** _____ **the time.** (forget, forgets)

7 **The owner** _____ **the door.** (lock, locks)

8 **The friends** _____ **on the window.** (bang, bangs)

9 **Many people** _____ **for help.** (call, calls)

10 **Finally the monkeys** _____ **the door open.**
(hear, hears)

Scholastic

In each row, give the number that comes next.

1.	2	4	6	8	10	12	14	16	
2.	1	3	1	3	1	3	1	3	
3.	1	2	3	4	5	6	7	8	
4.	1	2	2	1	2	2	1	2	
5.	0	6	5	0	6	5	0	6	
6.	2	4	6	2	4	6	2	4	
7.	100	101	102	103	104	105	106		

Scholastic

Add. Then color each box with an odd sum to help the boy find his way to the book. **Hint:** Remember to look in the ones place.

47 + 24	74 + 19	78 + 12	15 + 37
48 + 44	31 + 59	52 + 39	29 + 57	73 + 19
63 + 18	14 + 67	57 + 16	24 + 18	63 + 29
57 + 28	27 + 47	76 + 16	72 + 18	76 + 18
32 + 19	17 + 24	55 + 38	32 + 49	

Scholastic

Add. Circle each even sum to learn about George Washington.
Draw a square around each odd sum to learn about Abe Lincoln.
Hint: Look in the ones place.

A. the "Father of the Country"

$$\begin{array}{r} 423 \\ + 173 \\ \hline \end{array}$$

B. born in 1809 in Kentucky

$$\begin{array}{r} 384 \\ + 611 \\ \hline \end{array}$$

C. sixteenth president

$$\begin{array}{r} 325 \\ + 552 \\ \hline \end{array}$$

D. 6 feet 4 inches tall

$$\begin{array}{r} 257 \\ + 312 \\ \hline \end{array}$$

E. born in 1732 in Virginia

$$\begin{array}{r} 101 \\ + 561 \\ \hline \end{array}$$

F. studied geography

$$\begin{array}{r} 570 \\ + 408 \\ \hline \end{array}$$

G. first president

$$\begin{array}{r} 805 \\ + 163 \\ \hline \end{array}$$

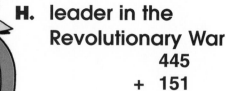

H. leader in the
Revolutionary War

$$\begin{array}{r} 445 \\ + 151 \\ \hline \end{array}$$

I. loved reading books

$$\begin{array}{r} 609 \\ + 290 \\ \hline \end{array}$$

J. leader in the Civil War

$$\begin{array}{r} 314 \\ + 183 \\ \hline \end{array}$$

Scholastic

Add to find the perimeter of each shape.

A.

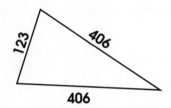

B.

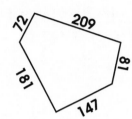

C.

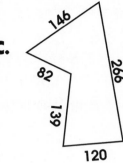

```
  1 2 3
  4 0 6
+ 4 0 6
_____
```

$+$ _____

$+$ _____

D.

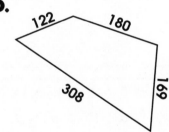

E.

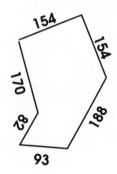

F.

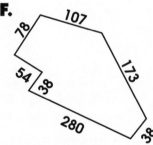

 $+$ _____

 $+$ _____

$+$ _____

Scholastic

Answer the questions.

Matthew plays the horn at different places. Last year, he played at 5 school events, 12 parties, and 7 baseball games.

1. At what type of event did Matthew play the most?	**2.** How many more ball games did Matthew play at than school events?
3. If Matthew had played at 5 more school events, how many school events would he have played at in all?	**4.** How many more parties did Matthew play at than baseball games?
5. Joe played at 10 events last year. Who played in more events, Matthew or Joe.	**6.** At how many different kinds of events did Matthew play?
7. At how many events did Matthew play in all?	**8.** At what type of event did Matthew play the least?

Subtract.

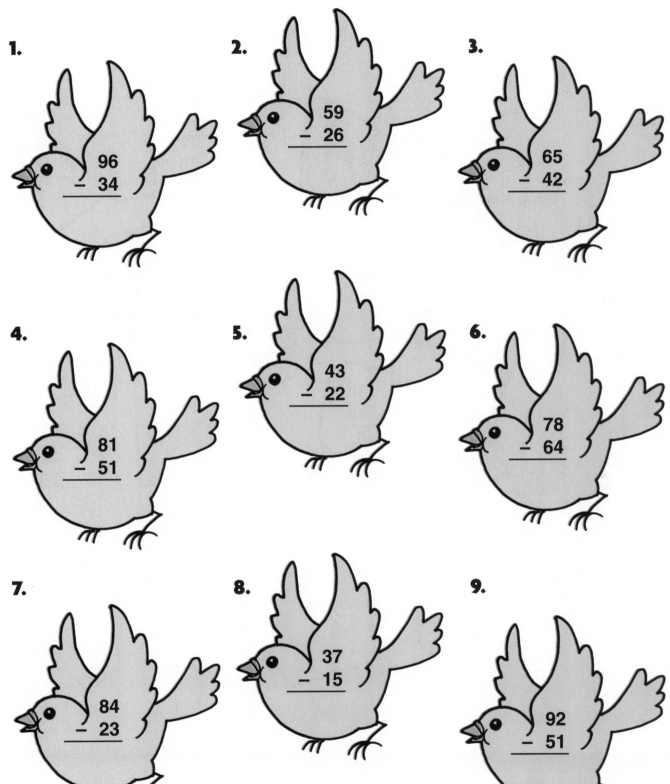

1.

$$\begin{array}{r} 96 \\ -\ 34 \\ \hline \end{array}$$

2.

$$\begin{array}{r} 59 \\ -\ 26 \\ \hline \end{array}$$

3.

$$\begin{array}{r} 65 \\ -\ 42 \\ \hline \end{array}$$

4.

$$\begin{array}{r} 81 \\ -\ 51 \\ \hline \end{array}$$

5.

$$\begin{array}{r} 43 \\ -\ 22 \\ \hline \end{array}$$

6.

$$\begin{array}{r} 78 \\ -\ 64 \\ \hline \end{array}$$

7.

$$\begin{array}{r} 84 \\ -\ 23 \\ \hline \end{array}$$

8.

$$\begin{array}{r} 37 \\ -\ 15 \\ \hline \end{array}$$

9.

$$\begin{array}{r} 92 \\ -\ 51 \\ \hline \end{array}$$

Subtract. Add to check.

65
− 27
38

38
+ 27
65

77
− 38
+

24
− 15
+

32
− 13
+

83
− 49

50
− 19
+

46
− 29

62
− 15
+

+

+

+

Old Town Pump

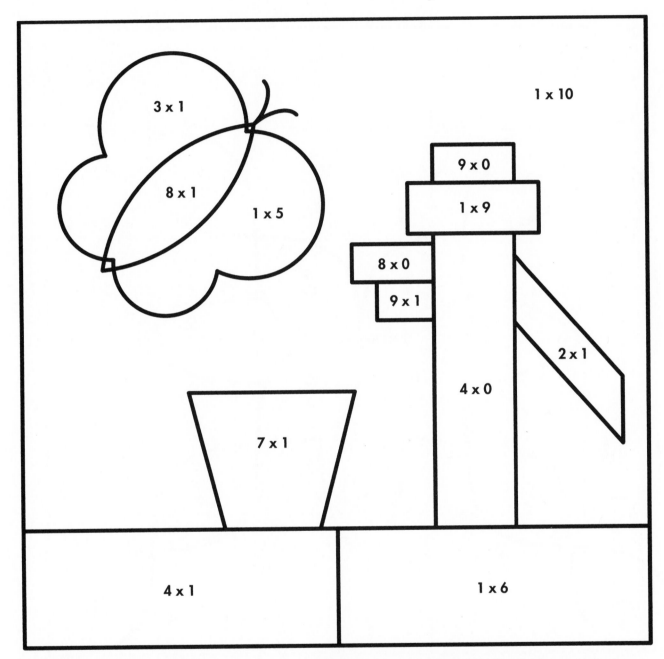

Color:

     0 and 2 = red
1, 3, and 5 = orange
    4 and 6 = green
  7 and 8 = yellow
        9 = black
     10 = blue

There was a time in the history of our country when people got their water from a town pump.

String of Beads

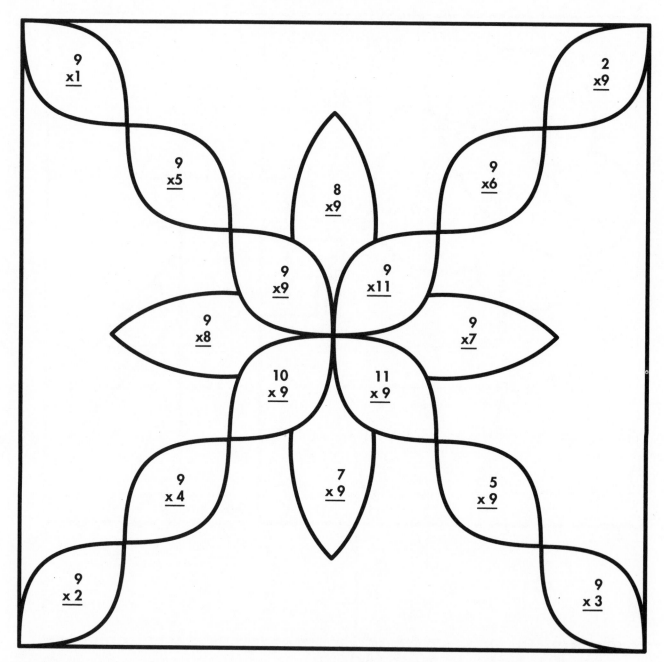

Color:

9, 18, and 27 = blue

63 and 72 = green

36, 45, and 54 = yellow

81, 90, and 99 = red

In pioneer days, people made their own beads out of wood or glass. Then they strung them into necklaces.

Scholastic

Mike's Afternoon Schedule:	
12:25	Eat Lunch
1:45	Go to George's House
3:15	Come Home from George's House
5:00	Take a Bath
7:00	Eat Dinner
7:45	Read a Book
8:30	Go to Bed

Write the activity that Mike has planned for each time shown below.

1.

_____

2.

_____

3.

_____

4.

_____

Scholastic

Circle the coins you would need to buy each item.

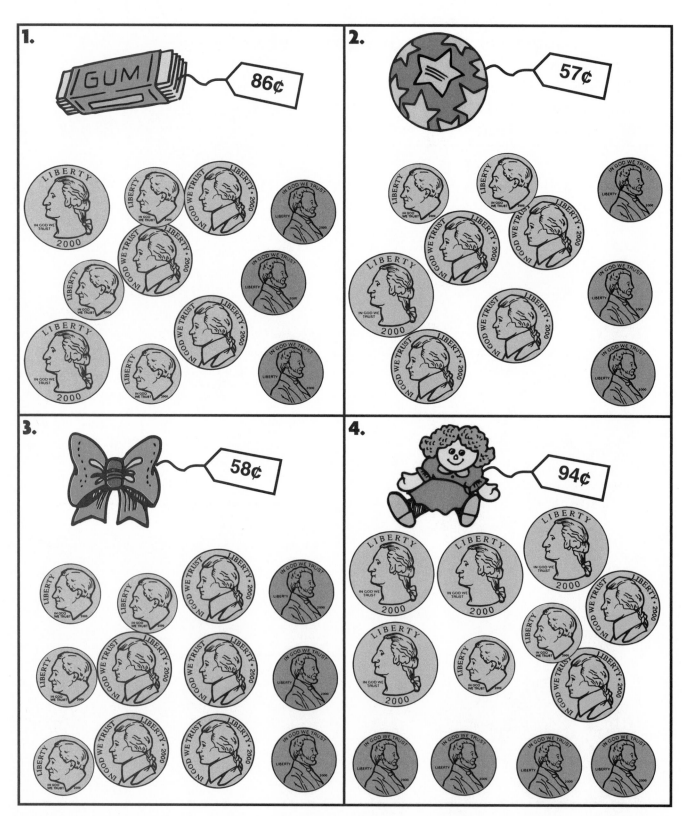

1. GUM 86¢

2. 57¢

3. 58¢

4. 94¢

Scholastic

Circle the set of coins that is worth more.

1.

2.

3.

4.

Use the chart to find what size each person wears.
Circle your answer.

1. Dale has a 28" chest. What size T-shirt does Dale wear?

Small   Medium   Large

2. Chris has a 27" waist. What size shorts does Chris wear?

Small   Medium   Large

3. Pat wears an 11" sandal. What size sandal does Pat wear?

Small   Medium   Large

4. Cam has a 24" waist. What size shorts does Cam wear?

Small   Medium   Large

5. Sam wears a 4" sandal. What size sandal does Sam wear?

Small   Medium   Large

6. Alex has a 34" chest. What size T-shirt does Alex wear?

Small   Medium   Large

Key
One inch can also be written as 1".

T-Shirts
(chest size)
20"–25" Small
26"–30" Medium
31"–35" Large

Shorts
(waist size)
20"–22" Small
23"–25" Medium
26"–28" Large

Sandals
(shoe size)
4"–6" Small
7"–9" Medium
10"–12" Large

Scholastic

Answer Key

READING/LANGUAGE ARTS

The Alphabet/
Manuscript Handwriting

Page 14–46
Review tracing, copying, and writing on each page.

Page 47–48
1. t   2. t   3. g   4. m and q

Phonics/Spelling

Page 50
1. c   2. a   3. e   4. f   5. b   6. d

Page 51
1. d   2. c   3. b   4. a   5. e

Page 52
horn, house, helicopter, hammer, hand, heart, horse, hose, hat, hamburger, hanger; EXTRA hide-and-go-seek

Page 53
vase, vegetables, violin, vest, vacuum, valentine

Page 54
kitten, kiss, key, kick, kite, king, kangaroo

Page 55
1. six   2. sun   3. flag   4. bread   5. bib

Page 56
1. cub   2. wig   3. pail   4. fox   5. leg

Page 57
1. sub, s, b   2. pit, p, t   3. net, n, t
4. lap, l, p   5. top, t, p   6. sag, s, g

Page 58
Review that directions have been followed and matching lines drawn.

Page 59
Review that beginning k, w, and r have sleepy eyes above and remaining letters are colored.

Page 60
3, 2, 4, 1

Page 61
1. fan   2. book   3. rake   4. log   5. fire
6. bell   7. ring

Page 62
hand: sand, land, band
ball: hall, call, mall, tall, wall, fall
dog: fog, jog, log, hog
cat: pat, sat, rat, mat, fat, hat, bat

Page 63
1. hill, crown   2. fiddle, spoon   3. clock
4. snow

Page 64
A. 1. an   2. and   3. as   4. had   5. at   6. can
B. Review   C. lamp, fast

Page 65
A. en: ten, end; et: get, let; other: red, yes
B. 1. red   2. yes   3. get   4. let   5. ten   6. end

Page 66
A. i: if, is; h: him, his; other: big, sit
B. 1. big   2. him   3. if   4. sit   5. his and is

Page 67
A. op: hop, top; ot: got, not; other: fox, on
B. 1. top   2. fox   3. hop   4. on

Page 68
A. two-letter: up; three-letter: but, run, bug, mud; four-letter: jump
B. 1. mud   2. jump   3. but   4. run
5. bug   6. up

Page 69
A. ay: day, play, stay; ai: rain, tail, wait
B. 1. wait   2. day   3. rain   4. tail   5. stay
6. play

Page 70
A. ee: tree, need, see, feet; e: me, we
B. 1. see   2. tree   3. we   4. feet   5. me
6. need

Page 71
A. i_e: like, kite; y: by, my, fly; shortest: I
B. 1. like   2. kite   C. by, I, my, fly

Page 72
A. o_e: home, bone, note, rope; o: so, go;
B. 1. note   2. rope   3. home   4. bone
5. go and so

Page 73
1. rude   2. flute   3. chute   4. dune
5. huge   6. June   7. cute

Page 74
flamingo, flag, fly, floor, flashlight, flipper, flute, flower, fleas

Page 75
Review that directions have been followed.

Page 76
1. glad   2. glider   3. glitter   4. glasses
5. globe   6. gloves   7. lip gloss   8. glue

Page 77
sneaker, snowflake, snorkel, snap, snail, sneeze, snout

Page 78
1. smoke   2. smile   3. smell

Page 79
1. stamp   2. stool   3. steeple   4. stork
5. starfish   6. stapler   7. stick   8. stove

Page 80
1. Twirl!   2. Twelve   3. Twister   4. Tweezers
5. Tweet! Tweet!   6. Twenty

Page 81
red: 1, 2, 3, 4, 5, 6, 9, 11; yellow: 7, 8, 10, 12

Page 82
Review that directions have been followed.

Page 83
A. begin with th: the, this, then, that; end with th: with, bath; B. 1. bath
2. then   3. that   4. the   5. with   6. this

Page 84
A. begin with sh: ship, she, shape; end with sh: fish, wish, brush
B. 1. ship   2. shape   3. she   4. fish
5. brush   6. wish

Page 85
A. begin with ch: chin, chop; begin with wh: whale, when, which; end with ch: inch, which
B. 1. whale   2. chop   3. inch   4. which
5. when   6. chin

Page 86
A. a: back, pack; e: neck; i: stick; o: rock; u: duck
B. 1. neck   2. duck   3. stick   4. rock
5. pack   6. back

Page 87
A. ar in the middle: hard, part, farm; other: are, star, jar
B. 1. hard   2. part   3. farm   4. jar, star, are

Page 88
A. 2–3 letter: or, for;
4–5 letter: corn, porch, horn, short
B. 1. short 2. porch 3. corn 4. horn
5. or 6. for

Page 90
1. C 2. G 3. B 4. C 5. H 6. B 7. B
8. G 9. B 10. A 11. G 12. C

Reading Skills & Reading Comprehension
Page 95
1. a good reader 2. looks at the pictures
3. the title 4. the words

Page 96
Clowns can do funny tricks.

Page 97
Trucks do important work.
Dump truck, cement truck, fire truck,
tank truck, flatbed truck

Page 98
A. KATE B. 1. brave 2. farmer 3. princess

Page 99
1. mice 2A. white 2D. woods 3. tail
4. run 5. bugs

Page 100
1. reading class
2. camping in the mountains

Page 101
1. pajamas, shirt, shorts, toothpaste,
toothbrush, hairbrush, swimsuit, pillow,
storybooks, sunglasses
2. grandmother, suitcase, toothbrush,
toothpaste, hairbrush, swimsuit,
storybooks, sunglasses

Page 102
6, 4, 2, 3, 1, 5   learn to dive

Page 103
1. My mother gave me some seeds.
2. I planted the seeds.
3. I watered the seeds.
4. Some flowers began to grow.

Page 104
1. I will put on my swimsuit.
2. I will jump in the water.
3. Grandma will fix lunch for me.
4. Mom will swim with me.

Page 105
1. We woke up early. 2. We ate breakfast.
3. Dad bought some bait.
4. Mom cooked our fish.

Page 106
Check prediction; Mia had to go to a
real hospital

Page 107
Check prediction; He knew he had to do
the right thing.

Page 108–9
Review that directions have been followed.

Page 110
Review lines and coloring;
red: books, crayons blue: blocks, marbles
Circle bacon and eggs.

Page 111
1. sandals, high heels, sneakers, boots
2. tickets, big screen, popcorn, candy
3. beans, peppers, burritos, tacos
4. tulip bulbs, fertilizer, gardening gloves,
pots

Page 112
meats: ham, chicken, roast
dairy: yogurt, milk, cheese
breads: bagel, muffins, biscuits
fruits and vegetables: carrots, corn, apples

Page 113
fast food; flower bed

Page 114
circle: hair, clothes, socks, shoes, bat/ball,
paintbrush/book
two lines: They are in the first grade.

Page 115
1. Juan's dad 2. Juan's dad 3. both dads
4. Ann's dad 5. both dads 6. Ann's dad
7. Juan's dad 8. both dads 9. Ann's dad
10. both dads

Page 116
It was a flying carpet. No

Page 117
1. True 2. False 3. False 4. True 5. True

Page 118
1. penguin 2. baby 3. octopus 4. ant
5. grandmother 6. bear 7. firefighter

Page 119
1. head cold 2. The children sneezed.
3. 9 4. She got a cold, too.

Page 120
1. Giraffe: Why do you have stripes?
Zebra: I don't know.
2. Giraffe: you should ask owl. Zebra: Yes.
3. Zebra: Why do I have stripes?
Owl: Ha Ha Ha.
4. Owl: Magic Fairy painted you that way!

Page 121
1. the cabin had no electricity.
2. the cabin had no running water.
3. she talked to her on the cell phone.
4. the cell phone was dead.

Page 122
1. E   2. B   3. D   4. F   5. A   6. C

Page 123
The worms got tangled up when they
danced. They were tied in a knot so they
got married.

Page 124
1–5 Review that directions have been
followed 6. the way she dresses
7. He wears his clothes backward.

Page 125
1. happy   2. worried 3. silly 4. sad
5. scared   6. surprised

Page 126
1. green   2. red   3. red   4. yellow
5. red   6. yellow 7. green

Page 127
1. uncle   2. yellow and blue   3. stars
4. me/the author   5. Yellow Bird
6. high

Page 128
1. king   2. fur   3. gold crown
4. Funville 5. a parade 6. yes

Page 129
1. three 2. two 3. one 4. Fifi and Foofoo
5. Hook 6. fresh food and water

Page 130
1. a frog 2. green with brown spots
3. in the pond 4. flies 5. flies
6. He hops around the pond.

Page 131
1. her doll 2. Kathy 3. blond 4. pink
5. sleeps on Karen's bed 6. no

Page 132
1. Chris 2. stories about stars and planets
3. the sun 4. pictures 5. a picture of the
sun 6. the sun

Page 133
1. the rain 2. raincoat and boots
3. outside 4. puddles
5. a duck 6. Meyer

Page 134
1. a dog 2. yes 3. brown 4. red
5. bones 6. to have a dog like Rowe's

Page 135
1. on her nest 2. yellow 3. eggs
4. They cracked open. 5. chicks 6. six

Page 136
1. a whale 2. blue 3. in the ocean
4. his whale friends 5. He jumps high
into the air. 6. He makes a big splash.

Page 137
1. B 2. F 3. B 3. G

Page 138
1. B 2. F 3. B

Page 139–140
1. A 2. G 3. B 4. C 5. J 6. C

Vocabulary
Page 142
1. start 2. happy 3. noisy 4. small
5. look 6. large

Page 143
down/up, little/big, out/in, girl/boy,
cold/hot, under/over, hard/soft, pretty/
ugly, happy/sad

Page 144
1. doorbell 2. football 3. sunflower
4. cupcake 5. beehive 6. bedtime
7. flowerpot 8. doghouse 9. popcorn
10. toothbrush 11. bookshelf

Page 145
1. hear 2. no 3. two 4. eight 5. scent
6. brake 7. sew 8. mane 9. rode

Page 146
1. triangle 2. square 3. diamond
4. circle 5. octagon 6. rectangle 7. circle
8. diamond 9. triangle 10. octagon
11. rectangle 12. square

Page 147
1. spring 2. winter 3. fall 4. summer
5. spring 6. winter 7. fall 8. summer

Page 148
1. blizzard 2. hail 3. tornado 4. rain
5. snow 6. sunshine

Page 149
1. penguin 2. bear 3. dolphin
4. octopus 5. alligator 6. pig 7. lion

Page 150
1. kitten 2. lamb 3. tadpole 4. duckling
5. fawn 6. cub 7. calf 8. piglet 9. chick
10. puppy

Page 151
1. doctor 2. bus driver 3. firefighter
4. dentist 5. teacher 6. librarian
thank you!

Page 152
air: airplane, helicopter
land: van, bus, car, bike, truck, train
water: sailboat, ship, canoe

Page 153
1. symbol 2. map key
3. north, south, east, west 4. compass rose

Page 154
1. west 2. maple 3. elm 4. south
5. north 6. east 7. ash

Page 155
1. responsible 2. honest 3. helpful
4. cooperative 5. kind 6. polite

Page 156
1. hard 2. arm 3. driver 4. yellow
5. bake

Page 157
1. write 2. bark 3. foot 4. low 5. circus
6. fish 7. eat 8. roar 9. down

Page 158
1. sweep 2. dark 3. big 4. full 5. cold
6. narrow 7. dirty 8. sky 9. sad 10. hump

Page 165–168
1. B 2. J 3. B 4. A 5. G 6. B
7. A 8. H 9. C 10. C 11. F 12. D

Grammar/Writing
Page 170
The, For, That, When, Have, Make, Could,
Are, Look, Go, This, Has, Name, Before,
Her, Where, The

Page 171
Review that sentences begin with a
capital letter.

Page 172
1–4 Review that periods are added at the
end of the sentences. 5. van. 6. red.

Page 173
1. The phone 2. My dad 3. Jon's hamster
4. Our bus 5. The teacher
6. Greg and Pete

Page 174
1. chases the cat. 2. hides the bone.
3. plays with a ball. 4. jumps in the air.
5. eats a bone. 6. sleeps on a rug.

Page 175
Color: We made a flag; The flag is big;
It is purple and blue; I hung it in my room.

Page 176
Review that sentences begin with capital
letters and end with periods.

Page 177
Review that directions have been followed.

Page 178
1. Run to the show!
2. Oh my, I'm very late!
3. What a great show!
4. Watch out, the floor is wet!
5. Wow, we had lots of fun!

Page 179
1. I like cats. 2. I see a man.
3. We go to school.

Page 180
1. This bear likes snow.
2. The water is cold.
3. The bear runs fast.
4. Two bears play.

Page 181
1–4. Review that directions have been
followed. 5. Review writing.

Page 182
1. Pam 2. Ant Hill 3. Ron 4. Bat Lake
5. Spot 6. Hill Street

Page 183
1. park 2. foot 3. ball 4. girl 5. net

Page 184
1. C 2. F 3. A 4. H 5. B

Page 185
Review that directions have been followed.

Page 186
1. sees 2. sits 3. mops 4. run 5. hops

Page 187
1. b 2. a 3. c 4. c 5. a

Page 188

Check answers make sense.
Possible answers: 1. am 2. were
3. is 4. gets 5. seems 6. are

Page 189

1. are, now 2. is, now 3. was, past
4. is, now 5. were, past

Page 190

1. was 2. were 3. are 4. is 5. are

Page 191

A. 1. looked 2. talked 3. waved
4. smiled 5. played B. played, walked,
jumped; Review sentence.

Page 192

A. 1. loved 2. asked 3. jumped
B. waved, talked, walked, jumped, asked

Page 193

1. kitten 2. bat 3. cracker 4. ball

Page 194

1. big 2. fast 3. bad 4. fat 5. fat 6. little

Page 195

Review descriptions to check colors and
patterns.

Page 196

Review that directions have been followed.

Page 197

1. long ago 2. yesterday 3. in winter
4. today 5. in the fall 6. last night
7. all day 8. at noon 9. yesterday
10. on Thanksgiving Day
11. this morning 12. Tomorrow

Page 198

Review sentences and that directions
have been followed.

Page 199

Review that sentences correspond with
the pictures.

Page 200

1. My Space Friend 2. A Big Beak
3. The Big Win 4. A Knight's Tale

Page 201

1. older: Beth, Carmen 2. taller: tree, bush
3. smaller: plant, tree 4. faster: fly, ant
5. taller 6. older 7. slower 8. bolder

Page 202

1. She, Kim 2. They, Kim, Joe 3. He, Joe
4. It, mango 5. She, Kim
6. They looked for mangoes.

Page 203

1. She 2. It 3. She 4. He
5. He 6. They 7. We

Page 204–207

1. B 2. H 3. C 4. A 5. G 6. A
7. D 8. H 9. C 10. A 11. J 12. C

MATHEMATICS
Addition

Page 209

1. 16 2. 13 3. 18 4. 17
5. 15 6. 19 7. 11

Page 210

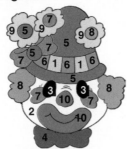

Page 211

Page 212

1. 3 2. 5 3. 2 4. 6 5. 3
6. 4 7. 6 8. 3 9. 6 10. 5
11. 4 12. 6 13. 3 14. 6 15. 5
16. 2 17. 4 18. 6 19. 0 20. 5

Page 213

1. 7 2. 3 3. 5 4. 7 5. 6
6. 7 7. 6 8. 6 9. 6 10. 5
11. 4 12. 7 13. 7 14. 7 15. 7
16. 4 17. 3 18. 5 19. 0 20. 6

Page 214

1. 5 2. 5 3. 10 4. 6 5. 10
6. 10 7. 8 8. 8 9. 9 10. 9
11. 9 12. 9 13. 6 14. 4 15. 9
16. 10 17. 8 18. 5 19. 10 20. 1

Page 215

1. 9 2. 8 3. 10 4. 8 5. 10
6. 7 7. 9 8. 3 9. 7 10. 9
11. 6 12. 9 13. 8 14. 3 15. 10
16. 9 17. 7 18. 7 19. 1 20. 9

Page 216

1. 11 2. 6 3. 10 4. 10 5. 8
6. 8 7. 9 8. 6 9. 11 10. 1
11. 10 12. 5 13. 8 14. 10 15. 9
16. 4 17. 9 18. 11 19. 11 20. 11

Page 217

1. 11 2. 9 3. 11 4. 10 5. 5
6. 6 7. 9 8. 10 9. 7 10. 8
11. 7 12. 10 13. 10 14. 10 15. 9
16. 11 17. 11 18. 9 19. 9 20. 11

Page 218

1. 7 2. 12 3. 10 4. 8 5. 9
6. 10 7. 12 8. 12 9. 8 10. 12
11. 12 12. 9 13. 11 14. 8 15. 11
16. 12 17. 11 18. 12 19. 11 20. 10

Page 219

1. 11 2. 12 3. 9 4. 12 5. 10
6. 12 7. 6 8. 9 9. 10 10. 7
11. 8 12. 10 13. 10 14. 8 15. 10
16. 10 17. 10 18. 9 19. 11 20. 12

Page 220

1. 11 2. 10 3. 13 4. 11 5. 12
6. 12 7. 12 8. 9 9. 13 10. 9
11. 8 12. 8 13. 11 14. 6 15. 13
16. 12 17. 9 18. 7 19. 9 20. 13

Page 221

1. 13 2. 14 3. 12 4. 12 5. 10
6. 14 7. 13 8. 10 9. 14 10. 13
11. 12 12. 13 13. 11 14. 13 15. 12
16. 10 17. 11 18. 14 19. 12 20. 12

Page 222

1. 7 2. 13 3. 9 4. 9 5. 14
6. 13 7. 7 8. 12 9. 14 10. 10
11. 13 12. 14 13. 11 14. 10 15. 11
16. 14 17. 10 18. 11 19. 13 20. 12

Page 223

1. 11 2. 13 3. 14 4. 12 5. 14
6. 14 7. 13 8. 11 9. 12 10. 11
11. 10 12. 14 13. 12 14. 14 15. 10
16. 12 17. 11 18. 13 19. 13 20. 10

Page 224

1. 11 2. 10 3. 13 4. 12 5. 14
6. 13 7. 10 8. 12 9. 12 10. 10
11. 12 12. 11 13. 15 14. 10 15. 9
16. 14 17. 9 18. 14 19. 14 20. 11

Page 225

1. 12 2. 15 3. 11 4. 12 5. 10
6. 11 7. 11 8. 14 9. 13 10. 17
11. 16 12. 12 13. 14 14. 17 15. 14
16. 13 17. 10 18. 10 19. 10 20. 15

Scholastic

Page 226

1. 15	2. 11	3. 12	4. 14	5. 10
6. 11	7. 13	8. 10	9. 12	10. 18
11. 10	12. 14	13. 17	14. 13	15. 12
16. 13	17. 16	18. 9	19. 14	20. 16

Page 227

1. 12	2. 18	3. 16	4. 11	5. 15
6. 18	7. 14	8. 10	9. 14	10. 13
11. 18	12. 16	13. 15	14. 14	15. 13
16. 11	17. 17	18. 10	19. 11	20. 16

Page 228

7 leaps

Page 229

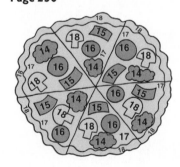

Page 230

Page 231

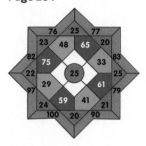

Page 232

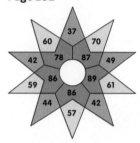

Page 233

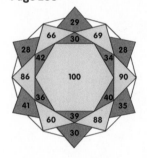

Page 234

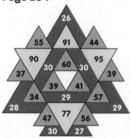

Page 235

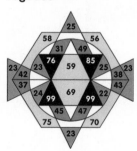

Page 236–238

1. B	2. F	3. C	4. G	5. B
6. H	7. A	8. F	9. C	10. G
11. C	12. J			

Subtraction
Page 240

1. 4	2. 2	3. 2	4. 4	5. 4
6. 0	7. 1	8. 3	9. 3	10. 3
11. 0	12. 5	13. 0	14. 1	15. 3
16. 1	17. 6	18. 3	19. 2	20. 3

Page 241

1. 3	2. 1	3. 2	4. 2	5. 2
6. 5	7. 0	8. 0	9. 3	10. 4
11. 4	12. 5	13. 0	14. 1	15. 6
16. 3	17. 5	18. 3	19. 1	20. 1

Page 242

1. 1	2. 3	3. 5	4. 0	5. 5
6. 6	7. 4	8. 2	9. 7	10. 3
11. 3	12. 4	13. 2	14. 4	15. 1
16. 0	17. 4	18. 0	19. 1	20. 2

Page 243

1. 6	2. 6	3. 1	4. 4	5. 1
6. 2	7. 3	8. 2	9. 1	10. 7
11. 1	12. 5	13. 2	14. 6	15. 4
16. 0	17. 3	18. 4	19. 5	20. 0

Page 244

1. 1	2. 0	3. 4	4. 2	5. 3
6. 0	7. 3	8. 0	9. 0	10. 6
11. 5	12. 4	13. 3	14. 4	15. 8
16. 0	17. 7	18. 2	19. 2	20. 1

Page 245

1. 6	2. 3	3. 4	4. 7	5. 1
6. 6	7. 2	8. 4	9. 1	10. 4
11. 4	12. 5	13. 5	14. 7	15. 8
16. 3	17. 7	18. 6	19. 8	20. 4

Page 246

1. 0	2. 2	3. 0	4. 5	5. 2
6. 6	7. 3	8. 3	9. 5	10. 9
11. 5	12. 6	13. 7	14. 1	15. 7
16. 7	17. 0	18. 0	19. 8	20. 4

Page 247

1. 3	2. 4	3. 8	4. 3	5. 1
6. 3	7. 4	8. 1	9. 10	10. 4
11. 6	12. 1	13. 6	14. 5	15. 2
16. 6	17. 4	18. 8	19. 3	20. 4

Page 248

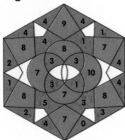

Page 249

1.3	2.6	3.4	4.4	5.2
6.4	7.7	8.9	9.3	10.9
11.3	12.2	13.2	14.1	15.3
16.8	17.1	18.2	19.10	20.7

Page 250

1.7	2.6	3.2	4.5	5.4
6.8	7.9	8.6	9.2	10.4
11.6	12.5	13.6	14.7	15.1
16.1	17.3	18.3	19.8	20.6

Page 251

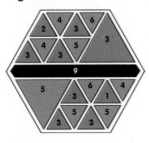

Page 252

1.6	2.4	3.9	4.7	5.6
6.6	7.5	8.4	9.8	10.9
11.5	12.9	13.2	14.6	15.3
16.4	17.5	18.8	19.7	20.7

Page 253

1.5	2.8	3.4	4.7	5.6
6.8	7.7	8.7	9.5	10.8
11.6	12.5	13.4	14.1	15.5
16.3	17.6	18.6	19.9	20.9

Page 254

1.6	2.4	3.9	4.8	5.4
6.6	7.5	8.1	9.7	10.6
11.9	12.7	13.4	14.6	15.8
16.10	17.8	18.5	19.7	20.8

Page 255

| A. 4 | B. 6 | C. 10 | D. 9 | E. 7 |
| F. 2 | G. 5 | H. 8 | I. 3 | J. 1 |

K. $5 - 2 = 3$ L. $9 - 3 = 6$
M. $7 - 5 = 2$ N. $8 - 1 = 7$
O. $12 - 6 = 6$ P. $16 - 8 = 8$
Q. $14 - 5 = 9$

Page 256

1.6	2.9	3.4	4.6	5.2
6.7	7.8	8.3	9.5	10.9
11.9	12.4	13.8	14.8	15.8
16.6	17.8	18.7	19.3	20.9

Page 257

1.8	2.2	3.8	4.8	5.9
6.4	7.8	8.5	9.9	10.6
11.7	12.9	13.5	14.6	15.1
16.8	17.6	18.3	19.9	20.7

Page 258

1.4	2.8	3.2	4.8	5.5
6.8	7.8	8.9	9.3	10.6
11.8	12.1	13.6	14.6	15.8
16.6	17.3	18.7	19.9	20.7

Page 259

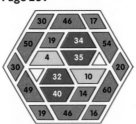

Page 260

Page 261

Page 262

$7 + 2 = 9 - 4 = 5 - 3 = 2 + 9 = 11 + 5 = 16 - 8 = 8 + 4 = 12 + 6 = 18 - 9 = 9 + 1 = 10 + 4 = 14 - 8 = 6 + 2 = 8 + 3 = 11 - 3 = 8$;
$12 - 3 = 9 - 6 = 3 + 2 = 5 + 9 = 14 - 6 = 8 + 7 = 15 - 6 = 9 + 3 = 12 - 2 = 10 + 7 = 17 + 1 = 18 - 11 = 7 - 5 = 2 + 13 = 15 - 7 = 8 + 3 = 11$; Car 2 wins the race.

Page 263

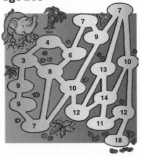

Page 264

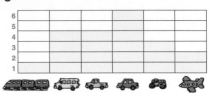

B. $3 + 1 = 4$ C. $6 - 4 = 2$

Page 265

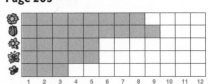

A. tulip B. $8 + 9 = 17$ C. $5 - 5 = 0$
D. $5 + 3 = 8$ E. $5 - 3 = 2$ F. $9 + 5 = 14$

Page 266–269

1. A 2. H 3. D 4. F 5. B 6. J 7. A
8. G 9. B 10. G 11. B 12. H 13. A
14. J 15. C 16. F

Time & Money
Page 271–275

1. 12:00, 6:00, 7:00; 12:00
2. 10:00, 11:00, 12:00; 11:00
3. 4:00, 8:00, 12:00; 4:00
4. 12:00, 8:00, 9:00; 9:00
5. 8:00, 4:00, 12:00; 4:00
6. 12:00, 6:00, 1:30; 12:00
7. 1:00, 2:00, 3:00; 2:00
8. 2:30, 3:00, 2:00; 2:30
9. 3:05, 9:05, 3:30; 3:30
10. 9:30, 12:00, 6:00, 2:00; 6:00

Page 276–280
1. a dime/10 cents 2. 3 pennies/3 cents
3. a nickel/5 cents 4. a nickel/ 5 cents
5. 2 cents/2 pennies 6. 3 nickels/15 cents
7. a nickel /5 cents 8. 2 dimes
9. 1 dime, 1 nickel, 1 penny/16 cents,
10. 4 nickels/20 cents

Page 281–282
1. C 2. G 3. A 4. C 5. G 6. B

GET READY FOR GRADE 2
Page 284–286
Review tracing and writing.

Page 287
1. shelf 2. hive 3. ground 4A. bath
4D. bed 5. finger 6. flower 7. lid
8. plane 9. brush 10. knob 11. farm
12. down 13. walk 14. cake 15. ball

Page 288
1. small 2. outside 3. apart 4. leave
5. stand 6. worse 7. light 8. all

Page 289
1. only 2. keep 3. forest 4. tired
5. happy 6. smelled 7. ripped 8. talked

Page 290
1. dear, deer   2. to, two
3. son, son   4. cent, scent
5. chilly, chilly   6. there, there
7. no, no   8. hare, hair
9. we, wee   10. hear, hear
11. wait, weight   12. brake, break

Page 291
1. anthers 2. stigma 3. petals 4. style
5. ovary 6. petals 7. stigma 8. anthers
9. ovary 10. style

Page 292

```
F I R E F I G H T E R D
A S D R E P W C Q T F O
B A K E R I M A L E A C
X C V B N L P P K A R T
C H E F O O I T J C M O
E R T Y U T Z A H H E R
D E N T I S T I G E R D
L A W Y E R J N F R A S
```

Page 293
1. B   2. A   3. B   4. A
5. C   6. A   7. B   8. C

Page 294
1. spots   2. seabird
3. a green stone   4. flute player

Page 295
1. both 2. Kendra 3. Lacey 4. Lacey
5. both 6. Lacey 7. Lacey 8. Kendra
9. Lacey 10. Kendra 11. Lacey

Page 296
People: doctor, aunt, boy
Places: village, office, school
Things: cane, pencil, bed

Page 297
1. present 2. present 3. present
4. present 5. past 6. past
7. past 8. past

Page 298
2. "That's a great idea."
3. "What should we bring?"
4. "We should bring food."
5. "Yes, let's bring lots and lots of food."
6. "You're no help at all!"
7–9 Review sentences for content and
quotation marks.

Page 299
1. writes 2. meets 3. ride 4. shop
5. closes 6. forget 7. locks 8. bang
9. call 10. hear

Page 300
1. 18 2. 1 3. 9 4. 2 5. 5 6. 6 7. 107

Page 301
47 + 24 = 71; 74 + 19 = 93; 78 + 12 = 90
15 + 37 = 52; 48 + 44 = 92; 31 + 59 = 90
52 + 39 = 91; 29 + 57 = 86; 73 + 19 = 92
63 + 18 = 81; 14 + 67 = 81; 57 + 16 = 73
24 + 18 = 42; 63 + 29 = 92; 57 + 28 = 85
27 + 47 = 74; 76 + 16 = 92; 72 + 18 = 90
76 + 18 = 94; 32 + 19 = 51; 17 + 24 = 41
55 + 38 = 93; 32 + 49 = 81

Page 302
A. 596 B. 995   C. 877   D. 569
E. 662 F. 978   G. 968   H. 596
I. 899 J. 497
Circle: AEFGH   Square: BCDIJ

Page 303
A. 935 B. 690   C. 753   D. 779
5. 841 F. 846

Page 304
1. parties 2. 2 3. 10 4. 5 5. Matthew
6. 3 7. 24 8. school events

Page 305
1. 62 2. 33 3. 23 4. 30 5. 21 6. 14
7. 61 8. 22 9. 41

Page 306

Page 307

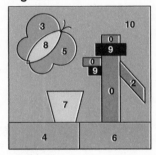

Page 308

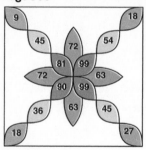

Page 309
1. Eat Dinner; 2. Come Home from
George's House; 3. Eat Lunch; 4. Go to Bed

Page 310
Review to see that coins add up to proper
amount.

Page 311
1. top (87 cents) 2. bottom (41 cents)
3. bottom (82 cents) 4. top (65 cents)

Page 312
1. medium 2. large 3. large 4. medium
5. small 6. large

Scholastic

Success with Reading & Math!

You're a Scholastic Superstar!

has completed the
Scholastic Reading & Math
Grade 1 Jumbo Workbook.

Presented on

Congratulations!

Totally Terrific!

STAR STUDENT!

GOOD WORK!

1ST PLACE!

NICE WORK!

SUPER STUDENT!

¡Perfecto!

Much Better!

TERRIFIC!

You've Got It!

BRILLIANT!

Way to Go!

Good Effort!

SUPER DUPER!

YES!

GOOD WORK!

LOOKIN' GOOD!

YOU DID IT!

¡MARAVILLOSO!

NEAT WORK!

SUPER

AWESOME!

NICE AND NEAT!

Way To Go!

1st Rate!

Star Quality!

DAZZLING!

SUPER!

¡EXCELENTE!

YES! WOW!

WOW!

YOU DID IT!

#1!

SUPER

YES! Doing Great!

So Proud!

Perfect Work!

¡Fabuloso!

CLASS ACT!

HARD WORKER!

GRRREAT!

GREAT GOING!

¡BRAVO!

WRITE ON!